Annual Indonesia Lecture Series
number 30

The return to constitutional democracy in Indonesia

Editor: Thomas Reuter

Monash Asia Institute
Caulfield

Monash University Press
Monash University
Victoria 3145
Australia

www.monash.edu.au/mai

© Monash Asia Institute 2010
The authors retain ownership of intellectual property for their own chapters

National Library of Australia cataloguing-in-publication data:

Title: The return to constitutional democracy in Indonesia : / editor, Thomas Reuter

ISBN: 9781876924652 (pbk.)

Series: Annual Indonesia lecture series

Notes Bibliography.

Subjects: Democracy--Indonesia.
Financial crises--Indonesia.
Indonesia--Politics and government--1966-1998.
Indonesia--Politics and government--1998-
Indonesia--Social conditions.

Other Authors/Contributors: Reuter, Thomas Anton.

Dewey Number: 320.9598

Printed by APS Print, Nunawading, Victoria, Australia.

Contents

Contributors iv

Indonesia's political and cultural transformation 1
Thomas Reuter

Explaining Habibie's interregnum 9
Irman G Lanti

Raising expectations: the Wahid presidency, and Indonesia's
democratic transition 23
Greg Barton

Megawati and the legacy of Sukarno 37
Angus McIntyre

The bearable lightness of democracy 51
Ariel Heryanto

The incredible shrinking Pancasila: nationalist propaganda and
the missing ideological legacy of Suharto 65
Robert Cribb

Winning hearts and minds? Religion and politics in post-Suharto
Indonesia 77
Thomas Reuter

Disdained but indispensable: political parties in post-Suharto Indonesia ... 89
Dirk Tomsa

Bibliography 105

About the contributors

Greg Barton joined Monash University as the *Herb Feith Research Professor for the Study of Indonesia* in January 2007. His knowledge of Indonesian politics and society, especially of the role of Islam as both a constructive and a disruptive force, is internationally recognised. In particular he is known for his work on progressive Islamic thought and its contribution to civil society and politics, but also his work on radical Islamist groups.

Robert Cribb is Senior Fellow in Indonesian History at the Australian National University. His research interests include mass violence, national identity, historical geography and environmental politics. He is the author of the widely used *Historical atlas of Indonesia* (2000).

Ariel Heryanto is Associate Professor of Indonesian Studies and Head of the Southeast Asia Centre at the Australian National University. He is the author of *State terrorism and political identity in Indonesia: fatally belonging* (2006), editor of *Popular culture in Indonesia: fluid identities in post-authoritarian politics* (2008), and co-editor of *Challenging authoritarianism in Southeast Asia; comparing Indonesia and Malaysia* (2003).

Irman G Lanti is the Program Manager, Deepening Democracy, in the Governance Unit of the United Nations Development Program Indonesia. His most recent English publications include 'Indonesia: accomplishments amidst challenges' in Singh and Salazar (eds), *Southeast Asian affairs* (2006), and 'Indonesia in triangular relations with China and the United States', in Simon and Goh (eds), *China, the United States, and Southeast Asia* (2007).

Angus McIntyre is an honorary associate at La Trobe University and the author of *The Indonesian Presidency: the shift from personal toward constitutional rule* (2005).

Thomas Reuter is a senior research fellow at Monash University in the School of Social and Political Inquiry. His research in Bali and more recently in Java has focused prominently on the anthropology of religion, status systems and cultural politics. Thomas has written several books, including *Custodians of the sacred mountains* (2002), *The house of our Ancestors* (2002), *Inequality and crisis in Indonesia* (2003) and *Global trends in religion* (2008).

Dirk Tomsa is a lecturer in the School of Asian Languages and Studies at the University of Tasmania. His research interests include Indonesian electoral and party politics, local politics and post-conflict reconciliation in Eastern Indonesia, as well as comparative Southeast Asian politics. He is the author of *Party politics and democratization in Indonesia: Golkar in the post-Suharto era* (2008), and his works have been published in journals such as *Indonesia* and *Contemporary Southeast Asia*.

chapter one
Indonesia's political and cultural transformation

Thomas Reuter

Since the fall of the authoritarian regime of President Suharto in 1998, in what is known as *reformasi*, or 'the reform period', Indonesia's political system has experienced tremendous democratic change. From a formal perspective, the political system has been transformed almost beyond recognition. In this volume, a group of international experts on Indonesian politics and culture retrace some of the main steps on this journey to democracy, highlighting the dramatic improvements achieved to date by the four administrations since Suharto's regime, but also drawing attention to continuities and a number of serious obstacles that remain in place and may yet derail or undermine democracy, equality and political freedom in Indonesia. Indonesians had lived under a condition of such deeply entrenched political oppression, where all authority rested with the President, his military support base and the monolithic state-party apparatus of Suharto's Golkar party and where open opposition was violently suppressed, that the events of 1998 came as a surprise even to seasoned Indonesia watchers. The speed with which the so-called New Order regime lost its stranglehold on the will of a population made compliant for an entire generation was astonishing, even against an historical backdrop of declining living standards in the wake of the Asian economic crisis of 1997 which was often credited as having triggered its demise. It was indeed easy to find reasons to be sceptical of the capacity of politically inexperienced reformers in the pro-democracy alliance to rebuild an authoritarian state in the image of democracy. But widespread fears that the reform movement would fall victim to political fragmentation, violent civil unrest and renewed military intervention were unfounded. While the reform movement did encounter a range of serious challenges, some predicted and others, such as the transformation of world political discourses after 11 September 2001, unforeseeable, it also gained unexpected support from within the establishment, most notably from Suharto's former Vice-President Habibie during his brief interregnum, and thus managed to press ahead with its agenda for democracy.The national, provincial and district legislative elections in 1999 and 2004 were generally fair, free and peaceful, as were the first presidential elections in 2004 and the parliamentary and presidential elections of 2009. With new decentralisation laws enacted in 1999, public service delivery and budget planning have been devolved to 450 municipalities and districts. The country held its first direct elections for provincial governors and district chief executives in 2005. Indonesians also have gained unprecedented freedom of expression, association and other civil liberties, as well as greater local political self-determination in the wake of comprehensive legislative and executive reforms, new human rights protection laws and the creation of a Constitutional Court. In election procedural and formal institutional terms, Indonesia has thus become a well-established democracy and it is now, indeed, the third largest democracy in the world. How well this democracy is functioning on the ground is quite another matter.

As Andrew Ellis (2005:1), head of Electoral Process in IDEA, pointed out,

> day to day governance, economic development, fighting corruption and building the rule of law is much less glamorous than building a new institutional framework after years of authoritarian government, but it remains the test of whether Indonesia will make democracy work.

Putting democracy into practice does not depend solely on the level of commitment to good governance and other aspects of democracy-building among politicians within the present and future administrations. Indeed, Ikrar Bhakti (2004:202–3), reflecting on this matter, concludes that such values were lacking among politicians:

> Many of the political elites state that they are committed to supporting democracy and reform, but in reality they practice the kinds of politics that demonstrate their lack of political ethics—ethics that are essential for the development of democracy.

Indonesia's political future may thus depend on the rise of a democratic culture at a more popular level, so that the public, civil society organisations and opposition parties will work together to hold any incumbent government accountable for poor governance and to press for further reform of institutions where change has been slow or partial, or where corruption remains endemic.

The failure to prosecute Suharto and his cronies, and, more recently, the acquittal of Muchdi Purwopranjono, former commander of Indonesia's special forces (Kopassus) and deputy head of the state intelligence agency, who allegedly ordered the murder by poisoning of human rights campaigner Munir Said Thalib on a Garuda Indonesia flight in September 2004, suggests that the judiciary has been and continues to be one institution where such cultural pressure for democratic reform needs to be applied. In the Munir murder case, amidst continuous media attention and public protests by human rights groups, the prosecution has appealed the decision with the Supreme Court. This case may be indicative of rising democratic pressures on all kinds of public institutions, rather than an exception. According to a recent report, cultural commitment to democracy in general appears to be quite strong and resilient in Indonesia now, at least within civil society:

> With the exception of fringe religious groups, all significant political actors and social groups appear to agree on the importance of democracy. Although there is some nostalgia for the levels of economic growth and stability achieved during Suharto's authoritarian New Order, no significant group argues for a government dominated by the military or the benefits of authoritarian rule. Moreover, Indonesians understand democracy to involve such basic ideas as open competition, protection of civil liberties, the rule of law, and respect for pluralism and minority rights. As part of this consensus on democracy, Indonesian actors agree on the importance of genuinely democratic elections and accept the premise that elections are the only legitimate way to change governments (Bjornlund, Liddle & Blair King 2005:4).

Indonesian's popular enthusiasm for democracy and general lack of nostalgia for authoritarian rule, rather ironically, is not shared by all international commentators, and the enemies of democracy may be found among those who most loudly claim to promote it. In 2005, for example, the *New York Times* published an opinion piece by Scott Atran, who wrote that 'the entrenchment of democracy has weakened Indonesia's willingness to fight terrorism... Such lack of resolve augurs ill for American efforts to promote democracy as an antidote to terrorism elsewhere in the Muslim world' (Atran 2005). Lex Rieffel (2008), via the Brookings Institution, even claims that 'in some countries, electoral democracy can be a recipe for political chaos', describing Suharto as a good friend of the United States who rescued Indonesia from the chaos of its first, post-independence democratic period in 1965. As for the new democracy under the current President, he notes that 'SBY [Susilo Bambang Yudhoyono] knows what needs to be done but cannot do it because he does not have the power to rule that Suharto had. In effect, right now, it can be said that Indonesia is suffering from an excess of democracy.'

Other commentators do acknowledge and welcome the advances Indonesia has made toward establishing democratic institutions, but they lament that, in practice, it is not the kind of democracy that serves the interests of ordinary citizens. Hadiz (2008), for example, argues:

> the problems that characterise Indonesian politics and society today—such as money politics, corruption, and thuggery—do not suggest any transitional stage to an idealised, liberal form of democracy. They indicate instead the essential dynamics of a way of exercising power that by now has become more or less established, and is likely to remain entrenched into the foreseeable future.

Although this pessimistic assessment of Indonesia's capacity to establish and maintain democracy may well be justifiable, these are hardly unfamiliar problems and we must exercise caution by interpreting observations about

'Indonesian problems' within a context of international comparison. Indonesia's problems are quite reminiscent, for example, of John Pilger's description of the underbelly of democracy and international diplomacy in nations like Australia and the United States.

Wherever we may choose to position ourselves in relation to these divergent opinions and perspectives, it is obviously unfair to compare the formal properties of Western democracies with the lived reality of non-Western democracies. And while a comparison between the formal institutional frameworks of different political systems may already be rather complex and difficult, it is even more difficult to obtain and interpret the information required for an objective comparison of the informal workings of democracy in different nations. On a formal level Indonesia has made enormous advances and would compare favourably on some counts to Australia, for example, by virtue of its human rights laws, because Australia does not have a bill of rights. But what about democratic practice? Hadiz, for example, in the article cited above, rightly criticises the continuing and sometimes violent oppression of trade-union activism in Indonesia. Even if we agree on the evidence, it can be difficult to draw a fair comparison. How, for example, do we interpret the deafening silence in the decline of organised labour protests following the dismantling of unions in Australia under former Prime Minister John Howard's neoliberal labour relations reform program? In order to put ideological commitments aside, one would have to ask what the real consequences of these policies were in terms of workers' wages and conditions. Vigilance and critical objectivity, it seems, are democracy's best friends in all parts of the world, and their work is never done.

Because of the dangers of looking at Indonesia's fledgling democracy through the distorting lenses of vested political interests and ideological positions, or from the diplomatic perspective of a particular geopolitical positioning, it is crucially important to provide accurate accounts of the realities of political change in Indonesia that are based on independent primary research. Such research, in my opinion, should be based on a balanced attitude of critical objectivity and empathy for the all-too-familiar human struggle for freedom from political domination as it unfolds among our neighbours.In my opinion, there are three important and closely interrelated tasks that lie ahead for those who wish to see democracy flourish in Indonesia. Political sector reform is the first, if not the foremost, of these tasks. Good governance, especially at the level of local government —now charged with providing many important services to the public—will indeed be essential for improving the credibility of the government and the proper functioning of daily life in Indonesia's local communities and in the business community. Resistance to practical democracy from local political elites is a major obstacle to achieving good governance; but there is also elite resistance at the national level. Perhaps the most significant challenge for democracy in the national political arena is the lack of transparency and public participation in the secretive inner life of the major political parties. The depth of the chasm between party elites and the public is reflected in survey results which show that political parties fail to reflect the aspirations of the absolute majority (65%) of citizens (see LSI 2007). The character of the parties is changing in a democratic climate, however, as they begin to depend more on media exposure than personal or identity networks (*aliran*) for gaining support (LSI 2008). This may provide opportunities for increased transparency, but could also encourage media manipulation by wealthy and influential candidates.

The second important task for Indonesian democrats is to strengthen the supremacy of the law, especially over politicians, public servants and business elites who would abuse their power, but also over cultural elites, including those who would impose their religious beliefs on others. The failure of the justice system to effectively curb corruption and abuses of public office has been particularly damaging to the credibility of all four post-Suharto administrations, though there have been moderate improvements under President Yudhoyono. The impunity with which civil society, religious organisations, such as the Front of Islamic Defenders, can violate the legal rights and the religious freedoms of other citizens is no different. The actions of the Front of Islamic Defenders, and also of combatants in Indonesia's numerous local conflicts, reflect the same disregard for a toothless and corrupt legal system and an associated culture wherein violence and criminal behaviour are considered normal.

Finally, the third task in the pursuit of democracy is a process of human capacity building and equitable economic development, driven by public education and health services. An independent public education system is essential if the next generation of Indonesians is to acquire the skills needed for effective democratic citizenship and for increased economic productivity. Human capacity building is the engine of equitable and sustainable economic development and will encourage the growth of the Indonesian middle class, thus providing hope and prosperity for many poorer Indonesians, for whom the measure of a government's success is still the price of kerosene, rice and cooking oil relative to their earning capacity, rather than the degree of their political freedom. Strong democracy thus requires and simultaneously encourages increased material prosperity and increased knowledge among citizens, as is reflected in the fact that the history of democracy in general is closely linked with the rise of the middle class and mass education. This interplay between democratic freedom, prosperity and knowledge is also central to the thought of leading contemporary economic theorist Amartya Sen, who sees economic and infrastructure development in terms of human entitlements and capabilities, and hence as a product of freedom and education (Sen 1999).

Outline

In this volume a group of internationally recognised Indonesia experts explore the terms of the five presidents of the *reformasi* period in historical sequence, the specific challenges they faced, their accomplishments, and their links to the legacy of the pre-Reformasi presidents Sukarno and Suharto. The final chapters look at two major themes within the Indonesian political scene during the entire *reformasi* period—the rising influence of political Islam and the ongoing struggle to establish a functioning system of political parties against a background of ethno-religious *aliran* politics.

In his chapter on the tumultuous early phase of democratisation, Irman Lanti explores some of the achievements of the Habibie administration in realising the aspirations of the Reformasi movement which had toppled Suharto after 32 years of authoritarian rule. Habibie's momentous decisions reflect an enthusiasm for political change that would seem surprising in view of the fact that Habibie had been Vice-President under Suharto and had come to power by default when the latter stepped down, rather than by riding the tide of the popular democracy movement. Dr Lanti sees Habibie's actions not as those of an opportunist, dedicated solely to his own political survival, but those of a modernist Muslim and representative of an outer islands (*seberang*) political culture that inherently favours a democratic political system.

Greg Barton, in his paper on the Wahid administration, argues that Abdurrachman Wahid or 'Gus Dur'—not unlike Habibie before him—was an unconventional choice for a political leader. Wahid was not a professional politician with a calculating and self-preserving attitude. Wahid took bold risks in his decision-making, rather than working to secure his own future as a career politician might have. Professor Barton suggests this may have been advantageous for Indonesia's still fragile democracy. Habibie and Wahid's risk-taking, idiosyncratic styles of leadership created a radical break with remnants of the power structure of the New Order and did not establish a new structure in its place. A new political monopoly or dynasticism was effectively prevented from establishing itself in the earliest and potentially most vulnerable days of Indonesian democratic reform.

Angus McIntyre reflects on the administration headed by Megawati Sukarnoputri, daughter of Indonesia's founding president Sukarno and leader of the most significant opposition party during the Suharto era. Dr McIntyre shows that, despite her timidity in public and apparent reliance on the charismatic memory of her father, Megawati knowingly departed from her father's legacy, most notably by supporting a separation of powers and a market economy. In opposition to her father's hostility to regional autonomy, she argued that such autonomy could be reconciled with Article 1 of the 1945 Constitution, thus providing Indonesia's emerging presidential democracy, and the amended 1945 Constitution that underpinned it, with a nationalist pedigree reaching back to the nation's founding father. Relating to the grievances of the Papuans, however, Megawati proved unwilling to compromise her father's conception of the Indonesian nation state, repudiating special autonomy and using a combination of force and divide-and-rule tactics in order to curb disaffection.

Ariel Heryanto then discusses the current government of Susilo Bambang Yudhoyono, a nationalist, former general of the armed forces and head of the Indonesian Democratic Party. In contrast to the generally pessimistic view among Indonesians and their observers alike, Dr Heryanto proposes Indonesia is now more liberated and democratic than has been generally acknowledged, but that an uncritical valorisation of 'liberal democracy' in academic and non-academic analyses can lead to the unwarranted conclusion that where there is democracy all is well. 'Democracy' has become the latest catchphrase in a discourse that has been keen to define what is lacking in Indonesia and reluctant to recognise that many of Indonesia's political problems are similar to those in the Western countries of the partipants of the discourse. In studying today's post-*reformasi* Indonesia, although it must be acknowleged that such problems do persist, it has become more difficult to maintain this conceptual distance.

Looking at events since 1998 with a longer historical perspective, Robert Cribb examines the controversial legacy of Suharto and of the nationalist ideology Pancasila which was largely discredited by the way it was employed by his New Order regime. Strong economic growth and relative prosperity may be remembered favourably by many Indonesians and foreign commentators alike, but Suharto's regime will be remembered more for its political brutality, corruption, the accumulation of crippling levels of national debt, and the stifling of free speech and discussion in Indonesia through censorship and intimidation. Given that his manipulation of the parliamentary and election systems and of the Pancasila concept was essentially hypocritical (being simultaneously a formal tribute to and an actual abuse of the values of democracy and national identity), Suharto's ideological legacy lacks any real substance. Cribb argues this is reflected in the events that surrounded Suharto's death in 2008. The absence of riots, disturbances and dogmatic reassertions of the values of the New Order suggests that his memory is quickly fading from the everyday reality of Indonesian public life.

In my own contribution, I discuss the role of political Islam, especially of Islamic radicalism, in Indonesia. I analyse Indonesian responses to the American 'War on Terror' and to a succession of terrorist attacks by Islamic extremists, from the 11 September 2001 World Trade Center attacks to the 12 October 2002 Bali bombing, and beyond, in order to determine the extent to which terrorist and anti-terrorist actions influenced popular ideas about the merit of political Islam as an alternative model to democracy during the early *reformasi* period, and into the future. Similar to Rizal Sukma (2008), I argue that mainstream Muslims have been strongly supportive of democracy and would predict that domestic terrorism, if it continues and if the government responds firmly without overreacting, will soon defeat itself by alienating the Indonesian public. At the same time, however, if the 'War on Terror' were to continue in a spirit of American unilateralism and neo-imperialism, then, for the foreseeable future, terrorists and sympathisers will be produced in Indonesia and elsewhere faster than they can be found and arrested. The latter scenario would appear less likely now, in view of the different foreign policy of the United States administration under President Barack Obama, who also happens to enjoy considerable personal sympathy in Indonesia. More broadly, the paper suggests that we need to examine more closely what it is that troubles Western observers about the rise of political Islam and whether that has anything to do with Islam's compatibility with democracy, for, as Jamie Mackie (2007:xii) has pointed out, 'if a democratically elected national government or regional authority enacts provisions of Islamic law that we dislike or deplore, we must remember that is something we [as democrats] just have to accept'.

Dirk Tomsa, in the final chapter, argues that political parties, even though they have, so far, contributed little to Indonesia's democratisation process, are nonetheless indispensable for the country's political future. While he agrees with many of the criticisms of Indonesian party politics, Tomsa concedes that the major parties deserve some credit for their contribution to Indonesian democratisation. The larger parties have not triggered so much popular discontent that a radical party could be established and they have collaborated and co-operated in parliament to produce democratic laws that make it difficult for potentially dangerous parties to be formed. Tomsa makes a number of recommendations on how Indonesian parties could improve their performance, both for their own sake and in the service of democracy.

Overall, this volume is designed to provide the reader with a balanced and multidimensional image of where Indonesia finds itself today in its struggle for a just and democratic society—a struggle which we all have reason to sympathise with.

chapter two

Explaining Habibie's interregnum

Irman G Lanti

In the final years of the 20th century Indonesia underwent another period of change in its political system. Similar to the changes of political structure in 1945 and 1965, this period was marked by bloody conflicts, confusion and uncertainty. Many observers were baffled by the speed and extent of change that swept the country. Suharto's power appeared to be so deeply entrenched in the Indonesian polity that only 'an act of God' (mortality) could remove him from power. Yet Suharto stepped down from power, and the political structure he had built over three decades crumbled.

From the perspective of Javanese political culture, Suharto's downfall was due to *pamrih*.[1] This *pamrih* took the form of corruption and cronyism that had become endemic, especially in the final years of his rule with the increasingly predatory business practices of his relatives. The practice of *pamrih* by rulers usually results in the loss of *wahyu*;[2] this was the case with both Suharto and Sukarno (Magnis-Suseno 1999).

This chapter will discuss, from a political culture perspective, *Reformasi* and the Habibie interregnum that defined the political set-up in Indonesia after the fall of Suharto. It attempts to explain why Habibie, regarded by many as Suharto's protégé, adopted a sharply different policy direction to that of his predecessor. While conventional wisdom had it that Habibie did what he did in order to survive the political transition process and keep himself in power, this chapter argues that Habibie's actions were informed by the politico-cultural environment that he hailed from, being a person from an outer-island tradition in Indonesia.

Habibie's politico-cultural background

In the Indonesian setting, important political segments are known as *aliran*. The definition of *aliran* is usually divided into two: the first definition is used more often in anthropological and cultural studies of Indonesia, since the concept was first coined in an anthropological study by Clifford Geertz in the 1950s.

The focus of Geertz's study was the divergent socio-religious practices in the Javanese community, between the syncretic *abangan*, the pious Muslim *santri*, and the aristocratic *priyayi* (Geertz 1960).

Political scientists Herbert Feith and Lance Castles expanded the concept of the *aliran* as political parties encircled by a number of social organisations, which are linked through formal or informal networks (Feith 1970). A number of studies have been undertaken using the political *aliran* perspective, especially in the 1960s and 1970s.[3] A further definition of *aliran* reflects its anthropological roots, but contains political elements. For example, Benedict Anderson (1990:fn85) refers to a unique, integral cultural outlook adhered to by a number of people with a similar world-view who are either organised or unorganised (but potentially organisable) in socio-political groupings.

In fact, the utilisation of the *aliran* concept by political scientists could be perceived as an extension of the anthropological perspective, as an attempt to gauge the saliency of the divergent socio-cultural groupings in the political arena. The political science use of the *aliran* could therefore be defined as structural, as it focuses more on *aliran* organisations and institutions, such as major political parties and associated major social organisations, whereas the anthropological use is more strictly cultural, focusing on the ideational aspects and socio-cultural practices.

It should be noted here that this division is not by any measure clear-cut. Analyses of political issues, such as the relations between religion and state, were given considerable attention even in Geertz's, *The religion of Java* (1960).[4] Feith's 'streams of political thinking' also dealt with some ideational analysis, albeit not to a great extent. Anderson's *Language and power* was perhaps the best work linking the political and the cultural in the Indonesian analytical setting. Nevertheless, there is yet to be a systematic effort at mapping out the relationship between the structural, embodied in political *aliran* groupings, and the cultural, in terms of general group perceptions, on statehood matters.

Anderson's work could actually be perceived as a beginning in this direction. However, it primarily covered only one facet of the segmented society—albeit the dominant group—the Javanese political culture and its manifestation in Indonesian politics. While significant and important, Javanese political culture is but one subset of Indonesian society; it shares the political space with other groups. These other groups who, for lack of a better term are known collectively as the *seberang* peoples, are spread throughout the archipelago (including the non-heartland areas of Java), which partly explains the difficulties in mapping out their political culture. However, they do have some common traits that eventually give rise to a discernible pattern of politico-cultural perceptions. It is important to note here that the role of Islam and its different modes of reception by different peoples of the archipelago, as well as its interaction with local tradition, also significantly influenced the politico-cultural traits of the *aliran* groups.

Modernist Muslims have roots in *seberang* culture. Many of the *seberang* societies, especially the more assertive ones such as the peoples of Sumatra and Sulawesi, are maritime-based. These societies tend to be more competitive and less obsessed with ideas of unity and harmony. The Hindu-Buddhist influence in these societies is also less pronounced than in Java, except in the notable case of the Sriwijaya Empire. Islamic influence is thus more significant in these societies. The *seberang* generally practise Islam in a more pure, orthodox way than their Javanese brethren. In the Indonesian political lexicon, they are known as the *santri* (pious Muslims).

Seberang political culture

In contrast with the vastness of scholarship on Javanese political culture, the political culture of the outer islands is inadequately covered, perhaps because the islands are spread across the archipelago, and are home to various groups. A relative lack of communication among them, unlike in Java, has rendered the creation of a single civilisation among these groups unimaginable. Hence, it is difficult to define accurately the presence of a *seberang* political culture.

Nevertheless, there are qualities common to many of these non-Javanese ethnic groups, or at least among the larger, more assertive and articulate ones. Among these groups are the Acehnese, Batak and Minangkabau of Sumatra, and the Bugis and Makassar peoples of Sulawesi, as well as the people of the Maluku islands. The people living in coastal towns in the northern parts of Java (*pesisir* Javanese) can also be classified within this group, along with the people of Banten (the westernmost part of Java).[5]

According to Koentjaraningrat, there are two categories in the socio-geographical features of these peoples. The first includes groups, the majority of which live in coastal areas: the Minangkabau, Acehnese, Buginese, Makassarese, the many groups of Maluku, and the *pesisir* Javanese. The second category includes other *seberang* ethnic groups that live in remote interior areas. Prominent examples of these are the Batak of Sumatra, the Toraja and Minahasa of Sulawesi, and the Dayak of Kalimantan.[6]

These two categories have something in common when it comes to the extent of influence from Indic religions, Hinduism and Buddhism. Compared to the vast Hindu-Buddhist influence in Java (and Hinduism in Bali), the presence of these two religions in the outer islands has been much less prevalent (Koentjaraningrat

1975:57–60).[7] As a result, social stratification did not become the main rule of the societies. While in many, if not all, of these groups there was a functional differentiation, especially the existence of rulers and followers, in general the differentiation was not as complex and intricate as in the Javanese model. In many of these ethnic groups, especially in the coastal communities, the rulers were less shrouded in an aura of mysticism and secrecy, and were generally more accessible. The decision-making process in the *seberang* communities was also generally more open and commoners were usually involved. The rulers frequently consulted the public in consultation meetings (*musyawarah*) (Sjamsuddin 1996:40–47; Effendi 1996:83–87; Sairin 1996:142–146).

The socio-geographical difference between the coastal and the interior non-Javanese societies did not amount to significant differences in their world-views about statecraft. In the interior outer-island tribes there was a significant degree of mysticism developed around the idea of power, but the lack of Indic influence rendered a relatively more relaxed social stratification. The coastal communities were traditionally engaged in commerce and seafaring activities. As travelling merchants, they tended to be culturally open, direct and individualistic. This was because of the relatively small amount of time they spent in their home villages, the sites of elaborate social customs and traditions. As a result, their fortunes were usually determined by individual rather than collective effort. Additionally, the *lingua franca* of the seafaring merchants in the archipelago in the 17th or 16th century was Malay. While the Javanese language was complex, the Malay language was comparatively egalitarian and less stratified.[8]

Because of the small agricultural surpluses and high rate of mobility of the people, the cultures of the *seberang* communities are less structured and elaborate (Liddle 1996:66). In some instances, the effort to develop classes of civil servants and nobility was interrupted by the strengthening of colonial rule. Such was the case of the Bugis, where the direct rule of the Dutch colonial administration made the use of symbols of nobility decline rapidly (Koentjaraningrat 1975:94–95).

Prelude to the storm

The storm of political change was brewing during the 1990s. Tensions escalated considerably in the 1990s; the number of mass actions and demonstrations, especially those related to land ownership issues, grew significantly. ICMI (*Ikatan Cendekiawan Muslim Indonesia*—Indonesian Muslim Intellectuals Association), which was established partially because of Suharto's desire to embrace the modernist Muslims in an effort to counter-balance growing criticism from the military, became increasingly critical under Secretary General Adi Sasono, who was elected in 1995. Through its think-tank, the Jakarta-based Centre for Information and Development Studies (CIDES), of which Adi was the director, ICMI made a number of bold statements in its seminars and conferences. The topics covered by CIDES' activities included issues deemed 'sensitive' by the regime, such as human rights, sustainable development and an equitable economy. At a CIDES seminar and later in one of its journals, *Sintesis*, M Amien Rais said that in the run up to the 1997 general election, Indonesians needed to think about presidential succession (Amien 1994). Amien was the chairman of ICMI's board of experts (*dewan pakar*) and a member of CIDES' board of advisors, as well as the chairman of Muhammadiyah (a modernist organisation and Indonesia's second largest Muslim organisation). This type of statement raised the eyebrows of observers and political players, Indonesians and foreigners alike, who had been certain that given its role as a political vehicle for Suharto, ICMI would never dare criticise the regime, let alone suggest a presidential succession when Suharto was in good health.[9] For this and Amien's other blunt statements in opposition to the regime,[10] Suharto pressured ICMI's chairman, BJ Habibie, long considered Suharto's *protégé*, to censure Amien. As a result, Amien was stripped of his position in ICMI's board of experts, but retained the CIDES' position.

Yet, aside from a few disturbances and actual actions against the government, there was no organised mass movement to demand change. Such relative tranquillity had, in fact, led the outside world in general to believe that Indonesia was stable, and that Indonesians were happy as a result of excellent economic growth performance. A number of analysts, such as Robert Hefner, argue that the key to Suharto's success in holding off any meaningful opposition during the last decade of his regime may have been the Islamic card he was playing. In the face of growing criticism from the nationalist faction of the military (the so-called Red-White faction), Suharto courted modernist Muslims for support. His blessing and active support for the establishment of ICMI in 1990, as well as the choice of his protégé, Habibie, to head the new organisation, could be seen in this light (Hefner 2000; see also Ramage 1995:ch3). However, there was a contending explanation for such a move. It is the cherished ideal for a Javanese person like Suharto to retire from the world of the mundane after reaching a certain age and to concentrate on 'preparation' for the afterlife.[11] The fact that he had been counselled by a modernist religious teacher from the army since 1987 strengthened this notion. As Suharto became more pious, the modernist community was at the height of a search for an alternative institutional affiliation.[12] The modernists realised from the beginning that in an autocratic set-up like the New Order regime, there had to be a patron from the government circle for any new association to survive. The result from the ensuing interaction between the modernists and the regime was positive for the former, not only because the regime approved of such an institution, but also because the approval came from the paramount holder of power.[13]

Whatever Suharto's initial intentions for ICMI might have been, subsequent events proved that he did use ICMI as a political platform. As ICMI and CIDES grew more critical of the regime, funding for CIDES activities was cut-off. Additionally, an alternative ICMI-oriented think-tank was set up. Known as the Centre for Policy and Development Studies (CPDS), the think-tank adopted a staunch pro-Suharto line amidst growing calls for reform. This think-tank was founded with the help of the president's children. At this time, Tutut (the most politically active of the siblings) and her brothers and sisters became increasingly suspicious of the modernists in ICMI, especially those affiliated with CIDES. They were also known to be not too fond of Habibie. At this juncture, Habibie had become the most senior minister in Suharto's cabinet. In such a position, he was not easily swayed by requests for projects or licences that came from Suharto family businesses. They also envied Habibie's 'strategic industries empire', which gave him the power to control a number of state-owned technological corporations, with assets amounting to trillions of Rupiah.

Before the 1997 election, the CPDS became more like a political operative seeking to undermine Suharto's opposition. Slowly but surely, ICMI was split into two camps: the loyalists led by the CPDS, and the increasingly critical camp led by CIDES. In the meantime, although now separated institutionally, Amien Rais maintained contact with a number of ICMI/CIDES activists. In Suharto's final days as President, Amien, together with other modernists such as Adi Sasono and M Dawam Rahardjo (a respected modernist scholar), played an important role in the *Reformasi* movement.[14]

If the relationship between some nationalist exponents, especially the civilian nationalists in the PDI, and the regime in this late New Order period could be described as adversarial, and the relationship between the modernists and the regime moved from reconciliatory to hostile, the position of the traditionalists *vis-à-vis* the regime took a different turn. The NU (Nahdatul Ulama, traditionalist vanguard institution) had been the most important Islamic organisation partner of the government during the latter half of the 1970s and 1980s in terms of propagating the policy of Pancasila (the state official ideology) as the sole foundation (*asas tunggal*) of all officially recognised organisations.[15] After the founding of ICMI, however, the relationship turned sour. The NU, especially its leader during this time, Abdurrahman Wahid, observed that the new Islamic organisation was heavily populated with modernists. Therefore, NU vigorously opposed ICMI's establishment. Even though the public position of Gus Dur (as Wahid is affectionately known) toward ICMI was that it represented a danger of the reintroduction of sectarian politics (Schwarz 1994:185–188; see also Ramage 1995:ch2), on a number of occasions he also referred to ICMI as a 'Neo-Masyumi' organisation. It appears that almost 40 years after the split between traditionalist and modernist Muslim organisations, the lack of trust between the two segments was still strong in the minds of their elite.

The NU also perceived Suharto's rapprochement with the modernists to be its loss. In an apparent balancing act, Gus Dur set up a rival to ICMI, known as the *Forum Demokrasi* (Fordem—Democracy Forum). In establishing this organisation, Gus Dur seems to have hoped to attract the nationalists to his side. Faced with increasingly strained relations with Suharto, the nationalists were naturally inclined to an alliance with the traditionalists. During the modernists' 'honeymoon' period with Suharto, Gus Dur's defiance served as a credible opposition, especially as it was backed by the NU, the largest Muslim organisation. As a result, in 1994 a number of political operations were carried out by the regime to unseat him from chairmanship of the NU and replace him with a figure deemed more favourable, a wealthy traditionalist entrepreneur named Abu Hasan. Unlike Megawati Sukarnoputri, Gus Dur survived this coup by relying on the support of most of the NU's respectable *kyai*.[16]

However, a couple of years later relations between the traditionalists and the regime took a sharp turn. In the run-up to the 1997 election, Gus Dur took advantage of the growing estrangement between the modernists, who became more critical of the regime, and Suharto, who increasingly came under the influence of his sons and daughters following the death of his wife in 1996. Gus Dur succeeded in establishing a good rapport with Tutut. At this point, Tutut became more active in politics. There were even reports that she was seriously considering running for the presidency. Gus Dur expressed his support for Tutut by referring to her as 'the future leader'. Gus Dur's pro-democracy activist friends were dismayed, but the political operation against him was halted. During the 1997 election campaign, Gus Dur and Tutut were hand-in-hand campaigning for Golkar.[17]

It was this intriguing political constellation that marked the end of the New Order regime. As mentioned above, the seeds for the resurgence of *aliran* politics were sown in this period. All three *aliran* segments were vying for power as Indonesia neared a post-Suharto era.

Habibie's interregnum

Professor Bacharudin Jusuf Habibie was a German-trained aeronautics engineer. He was born and raised in Makassar, South Sulawesi and therefore regarded as a non-Javanese leader.[18] He also had strong modernist Muslim credentials, which became an asset to his political advancement. His family became closely acquainted with Suharto during Suharto's time in Makassar as commander of the Mandala operation to liberate West New Guinea in the late 1950s and early

1960s. After completing his education in Germany in the 1970s, Habibie went to work at MBB (Messerschmidt Bölkow Blohm), a German aircraft manufacturing company. He was summoned by Suharto some time in the 1970s to spearhead Indonesia's research development in high technology.

Habibie's close relationship with Suharto was an asset for his career in the bureaucracy during the New Order era. He served several times in Suharto's cabinet as Minister of Research and Technology. By the time he became Vice-President in 1998, he was the longest serving minister. While his previous record as a modernist Muslim had been obscured, after 1990 he became closely associated with this segment when he was elected chairman of ICMI. He served in that position until his election as Vice-President.

Many analysts believe that Suharto chose Habibie in an effort to offset growing opposition within the ranks of the nationalist military and to cultivate support among the modernists. But a number of ICMI's influential members contend that the choice of Habibie actually came from their own initiative. They had previously identified Habibie as a pious Muslim of modernist persuasion. The fact that Habibie was also close to Suharto seemed to provide another incentive for the modernists, as they realised that no public or political venture could proceed without the blessing of the country's leader. It was said that Suharto gave his approval for ICMI's choice of Habibie afterwards.[19] In any case, Habibie's presidency marked the ascendancy of the modernists in Indonesian politics after a long period of obscurity under Sukarno's Guided Democracy and Suharto's New Order. A number of modernist leaders and 'green' officers entered the cabinet. Among the prominent figures were: Adi Sasono as Minister of Co-operatives and Small and Medium Enterprises; Feisal Tanjung as Co-ordinating Minister of Politics and Security; Syarwan Hamid as Minister of Home Affairs; Yunus Yosfiah, another 'green' general, as Minister of Information; ICMI's functionaries Muladi and Muslimin Nasution as Minister of Justice and Minister of Forestry and Estates respectively; the PPP's (an amalgamation of Muslim parties) Hamzah Haz and AM Saefuddin as Minister of Investment and Minister of Population; and Muhammadiyah's Malik Fajar as Minister of Religious Affairs. Habibie's presidential advisors (non-cabinet members) were also overwhelmingly made up of ICMI and CIDES figures, such as A Watik Pratiknya, Jimly Asshiddiqie, Dewi Fortuna Anwar, Indria Samego and Umar Juoro.

Habibie's presidency was characterised by a dualism of the desire for reform and the persistent practices of the New Order regime, especially with regard to corruption. It was also marked by the return of *aliran* politics that had been dormant during the Guided Democracy and New Order periods, including divisiveness and power struggles among the *aliran*.

Habibie's administration began by carrying out sweeping reform. He immediately ordered the release of political prisoners jailed during the Suharto era on charges of subversive activities, including those from the 1965 failed Communist coup attempt who had been in prison for more than three decades. He also repealed the controversial Surat Izin Usaha Pers dan Penerbitan (press and publication licence) that had shackled the freedom of the press. As a consequence, censorship on political reporting was lifted.

Most importantly perhaps was Habibie's offer to the parliament to revise the five political laws that had been the mainstay of Suharto's authoritarian rule. These laws were on elections, parliament, political parties, social organisations and referenda.[20] Also revised was an equally, if not more infamous law: the anti-subversion law.[21] As a result of the new laws, the public was now free to set up political parties. In less than a year, between May 1998 and February 1999, 160 political parties were established, far more than the three official parties that had been allowed to compete in elections since 1973. Also, the parliament could now play a greater role than it had previously. For instance, it now had the power to draft laws, whereas previously all bills came from the executive, and parliament's legislative role was limited to discussion and then adoption of the laws. Government officials, who previously had no alternative but vote in elections for Golkar, the government party, were now freed from this obligation. Elections would be organised by an independent KPU (*Komisi Pemilihan Umum*—General Elections Commission), whose members were now members of the public rather than government officials. It was also agreed that the next election would be a national holiday. This measure was taken to ensure that all voters would vote in their neighbourhoods rather than in their offices, where pressure to vote for a certain party had often taken place in the past.

Habibie decided that the question of East Timor, which had for so long impaired Indonesia's credibility in the international community, should be resolved as soon as possible. He first offered a special autonomy to the territory, but upon advice from the Australian Prime Minister John Howard, decided to offer the East Timorese a referendum to decide whether they would like to remain part of Indonesia under the special autonomy plan, or be independent. He also requested that the referendum be held under the auspices of the United Nations. It should be noted that some of the East Timorese freedom fighters, such as Xanana Gusmao, were initially reluctant to take up this offer. Gusmao offered Habibie another option in which East Timor would have under special autonomy for a certain period (up to five years), after which a referendum would be held. Habibie reportedly rejected this option, saying that if at the end the East Timorese decided to become independent, then the five-year period would be a waste of resources for Indonesia. The question, according to Habibie, needed to be settled quickly.

The referendum was held on 30 August 1999. The result was overwhelmingly (78.5%) pro-independence. This was met with violence by pro-autonomy militias, which were reportedly set up by the Indonesian military to campaign against independence. The level of violence reached a point where the international community demanded intervention. President Habibie relented by inviting an international peacekeeping operation to the troubled territory. The militias then drove more than 100,000 East Timorese to the neighbouring Indonesian territory of West Timor. Since then, the militias have often carried out insurgency operations in East Timor, and remain a thorn in Indonesia's side. Contrary to Habibie's hope, the issue of East Timor was not immediately resolved after all. Domestically, Habibie's handling of East Timor was met with disdain from many quarters, especially among the nationalist segment, both the party and military variants. It would become one of the political liabilities that eventually drove Habibie out of power.[22]

Another weak point also enfeebled Habibie's presidency. Despite political reforms undertaken by his administration, corrupt practices still occurred, especially those related to party financing by government officials using state facilities. The largest scheme was what became known as Bank Bali-gate. In order to finance the upcoming election, a number of Golkar functionaries contacted the officials at BPPN (*Badan Penyehatan Perbankan Nasional*—Indonesian Bank Restructuring Agency—IBRA) and Bank Bali, one of Indonesia's largest private banks, to offer help in collecting debt from interbank loans to a number of Indonesian banks. In return for the service, Bank Bali offered payment of a large sum, which was then channelled to Golkar. The deal was uncovered by an economist, and it became a scandal that marred Habibie's administration.[23]

In spite of delivering the promises of political reform, Habibie's administration remained largely unpopular, especially among the students and NGO activists. This, and other scandals, in which some officials in Habibie's administration were involved, seemed to confirm their accusation that Habibie was Suharto's protégé and an integral part of the New Order regime. Therefore, they stuck to their original demand of total reform, which meant eradication of all proponents of the old regime from government.

For segmental leaders, Habibie's administration was seen as a modernist government. They tended to see Habibie's ascendancy to the presidency as illegitimate because the election that formed the current parliament and eventually resulted in Habibie's election as vice president was carried out in the old era. The nationalist and traditionalist leaders used the image of Habibie as part of the old regime to mount a continuous attack on the modernist administration, in tandem with the ever-critical 'secular' nationalists, and this time also traditionalist students and activists.

Some prominent modernists, such as Amien Rais, continued their opposition to Habibie's rule, mainly because of Habibie's overwhelming public image as Suharto's protégé and his unwillingness to prosecute Suharto on corruption charges. Fresh from the success of the united movement to topple Suharto, Amien maintained a close relationship with the nationalist leaders. However, while he still occasionally criticised Habibie's administration, the extent of Amien's opposition was certainly a far cry from his tough defiance and unwavering stance against Suharto's rule that earned him the nickname 'locomotive of *Reformasi*'.[24]

Realising that his regime lacked widespread support, Habibie announced that his was a transitional administration and that the general election, formerly scheduled to be held in 2003, would be held in 1999. This election would be held under the new set of political laws, and became the first free, fair and open election in Indonesia since the 1955 election. Of the hundreds of political parties established initially, the KPU allowed only 48 to contest the election.[25] It was to be an election marked by the rebirth of *aliran*ism in Indonesia's political structure.

Conclusion

The modernists are generally more in favour of open political competition than the other *aliran*-based groups. The modernists are at ease with the idea of a dispersion of power. On the distribution of power among political parties and offices, they have greater affinity for the idea of competitive and oppositional politics than the other *aliran*. This *aliran* is not opposed to the idea of political competition through elections that result in an alternation of power; nor does it object to checks and balances among political institutions.

While the nationalist Sukarno decided that the rather chaotic political competition of parliamentary democracy was not suitable for Indonesia, modernist leaders, such as Natsir, had a positive perception of the system. And when Sukarno declared the change in the political system from parliamentary to Guided Democracy through the Presidential Decree of 5 July 1959, the modernists were clearly dismayed. They first initiated the Liga Demokrasi, with other parties, especially the urban-based PSI (*Partai Sosialis Indonesia*— Indonesian Socialist Party) and the *seberang* Partai Katolik (Catholic Party), as a protest movement. Later, some Masyumi and PSI figures were involved in the regional rebellions of PRRI/Permesta.[26]

After the banning of Masyumi in 1962, there was a long hiatus of modernist active political participation, a period that included the final years of Guided Democracy and the first and middle parts of the New Order. In 1990, with the establishment of ICMI, the modernists saw a chance to resume political involvement. While ICMI was undoubtedly a political vehicle of the regime looking for an alternative foothold, the views within ICMI on the state and governance were unmistakably modernist. During the period when New Order authoritarianism was at its prime, ICMI opened up a discourse on some issues considered taboo by the regime, such as human rights, the environment, demilitarisation, and an equitable economy. Some ICMI members even quite openly called for a presidential succession.

After the fall of Suharto, the modernists found an open space for political participation. During the interregnum period, Habibie, the former chairman of ICMI with a *seberang* modernist background, carried out a number of sweeping reforms of the system. While Habibie's administration was marred by corruption scandals and widespread opposition arising from his image as Suharto's *protégé*, he did initiate an opening up of the political system. Habibie's actions, therefore, can be read as logical consequences of his political-cultural background as a *seberang* modernist Muslim.

Notes

1 Roughly translated, this means a 'concealed personal motive'.
2 This means 'divine favour for power holders'.
3 See for example, the analysis of the influence of the *aliran* on the elite bureaucracy in Emmerson (1976). On the operation of *aliran* politics in the local level, see Liddle (1970).
4 See especially chapters 13 and 15.
5 The classification of the Sundanese of West Java is rather difficult. Due to their historical rivalry with the Javanese kingdoms, the Sundanese always insist that they are non-Javanese. However, to classify them as *seberang* is problematic because the extent of Hindu influence is equally extensive in the Sunda land as in Central and East Java, especially in the eastern part where the courts of the old Sundanese kingdom of Padjadjaran was located.
6 It is important to note here that some interior *seberang* ethnic groups were still living in a fairly simple, secluded style, and still practised certain kinds of animist beliefs (usually in combination with the practice of a major religion, most notably Christianity). This is especially true in Papua, as well as for some ethnic groups in Sumatra, Kalimantan and Sulawesi. Being situated in the margins of the country's social and political relations, they are less significant in shaping what is considered here as the *seberang* political-culture.
7 The high level of influence of Hinduism in Bali caused its people to share many similarities in political culture with the Javanese. The royal families of Bali originated in the Majapahit court, fleeing from Java during the power struggle with the Islamic sultanate of Demak.
8 The variant of the language used was *Melayu pasar* (market Malay). A more stratified variant is used among the Malay aristocracy, though it is not as complex as the Javanese language.
9 For details on the presidential succession debates, see Singh (2000:ch1).
10 Among Amien's other 'sins' were first, his fierce attack on Suharto family cronyism, especially the Busang mining project that involved the Canadian-based company Bre-X, and second, his declaration that he was ready to run in the election in 1997 as a presidential candidate.
11 Known in Javanese idiom as *lengser keprabon, madeg pandhito*. Suharto reiterated this intention on many public occasions from 1993.
12 Prior to ICMI's establishment in 1990, there had been a number of efforts by the modernists to set up similar institutions throughout the 1980s (see Hefner 2000:129–31).
13 Hefner provides the details surrounding ICMI's establishment (see Hefner:128–38).
14 With several modernist activists, they co-ordinated the mass movement from the headquarters of Muhammadiyah in Menteng, Jakarta.

15 For the reasoning behind the NU's acceptance of the *asas tunggal* requirement, see Feillard (1999:ch9). See also Ramage (1995:ch2).
16 For details on the political operation against Gus Dur, see Hefner (2000:171–4).
17 Hefner, however, argues that Gus Dur's move must be perceived solely as a political strategy to counter the modernists' ascendancy rather than signifying a change in his democratic ideals. See Hefner (2000:193–6).
18 He came from a family of mixed (inter-ethnic) marriage. While his father was a Buginese from South Sulawesi, his mother was Javanese. He was also married to a Javanese.
19 On the circumstances surrounding ICMI's choice of Habibie, see Hefner (2000:128–38).
20 The referendum law referred to any proposed alteration to the executive-heavy 1945 Constitution. This law virtually eliminated any way for the Constitution to be amended, since it required 90% of the population to participate in the referendum, and 90% of votes to agree to the proposed amendment.
21 Ironically, efforts to replace this law with a softer one were met with stiff opposition from the students and activists, who remained in opposition to Habibie's rule. Apparently, the more relaxed content of the law did not matter as much as who drafted it.
22 There are now quite a few eyewitness accounts of the referendum and the ensuing violence in publication. For a succinct account, as well as discussion of Indonesia's domestic circumstances surrounding the issue, see Emmerson (1999).
23 For details on Baligate, see among others van Dijk (2001:417–30).
24 Amien would also later create a distance between himself and the nationalists by not supporting Megawati's bid for the presidency. Eventually, Amien promoted the creation of a loose parliamentary alliance of modernist parties, the Poros Tengah (middle-axis). As its name suggested, the alliance was meant as a force to oppose the election of both Habibie and Megawati.
25 The selection was based on a regional representation principle, that a party should have the capacity to establish branches at least in half of the provinces, and it should also be able to establish branches in at least half of the districts in the province to validate provincial representation.
26 *Pemerintahan Revolusioner Republik Indonesia* (PRRI, Revolutionary Government of the Republic of Indonesia) was a rebellion against the central government that took place in Sumatera. This movement coincided with similar movement in Sulawesi, under the name of *Perjuangan Rakyat Semesta* (Permesta, Universal Struggle of the People). The rebellions are often lumped together because of their similar timing (1957–61), raison d'etre, the involvement of figures of Masyumi and PSI, and the support of the United States and its allies. The two movements were merged in 1958 when Permesta became part of the larger PRRI rebellion. For discussion on US role in PRRI-Permesta, see Kahin & Kahin (1995).

chapter three

Raising expectations: the Wahid presidency, and Indonesia's democratic transition

Greg Barton

Achieving good governance continues to be the greatest challenge facing contemporary Indonesia, as it remains much more the exception than the rule. At the same time, economic growth, although reasonably good, lags behind what is required to soak up Indonesia's considerable unemployment and underemployment and to lift the rate of poverty alleviation to acceptable levels. It is only natural, therefore, that when Indonesians look around they feel disappointment at the lack of progress and frustration because things are not better than they are. Consequently, when asked whether they are satisfied with the results of transition to democracy, many Indonesians will answer in the negative.

On the other hand, when external observers look at Indonesia, particularly when they compare it with other nations that have experienced regime change and democratisation, they are generally struck by the remarkable rate of progress over the last 11 years. Long-term observers of Indonesia are particularly struck by the rate. The turbulent late Suharto years are rapidly becoming a distant memory, but for those who can remember the discussions of the 1990s about what lay ahead for Indonesia in the post-Suharto era and about how costly, in terms of human lives and suffering, the transition would be, there was very little optimism that Indonesia could move beyond the three decades of authoritarian rule without paying a tremendous price. As it happens, whilst many individuals certainly did pay a tremendous price, the transition was nothing near as traumatic as was expected. The elections of 1999 and 2004 went ahead smoothly and peacefully, and Indonesia returned to the parliamentary democracy of the mid-1950s so naturally that it was almost as if the previous 40 years had been but a brief interlude. Even more remarkably, the Indonesian military returned to barracks, albeit more slowly in some provinces than others, and withdrew from practical politics at a pace and in a manner that few had dared hope for, much less predict.

One of the main reasons for the pessimism of the 1990s when looking ahead was that Indonesia continued to be characterised by a small middle class and very extensive poverty. Given that the size of the middle class and the extent and vitality of civil society are inevitably closely linked, it looked certain that Indonesia lacked the requisite civil capacity to ensure a peaceful and sustainable transition to liberal democracy. What happened proved these assumptions to be inadequate and based on an incomplete understanding of Indonesian society. It appears that part of the explanation for Indonesia's successful transition lies in the fact that it had a hidden and more extensive civil sector than had been generally understood, and that this underestimated civil capacity lay primarily with mass-based Islamic organisations Muhammadiyah and Nahdlatul Ulama (NU). Just as Iran's revolution in 1979 caught observers by surprise precisely because they had been looking for social uprising in places other than the mosques and Islamic networks, in Indonesia there was also a lot more going on in religious civil circles in the Suharto era than we had really recognised. In hindsight, it now seems clear that not only had Muhammadiyah and NU contributed to a peaceful transition by encouraging restraint and moderation, but they had also effectively been schooling tens of millions of Indonesians in democratic processes and principles through their own internal organisational mechanisms. At the same time Indonesia was blessed with a considerable number of Islamic leaders, some high profile and some relatively unknown, who encouraged people to understand democracy and democratic principles as being congruent with Islam and to recognise that democratic reform and general progressive concerns were very much the business of Islam. Leaders such as Amien Rais, Nurcholish Madjid and Abdurrahman Wahid were at the forefront of the Reformasi movement. It was men such as these who went into the palace to meet with the President in his final days and confront him with the fact that he had no option but to step down gracefully and peacefully.

There were many reasons why Suharto decided he had no option in the end but to step down. One of the reasons was that he felt that sections of society that he could count on previously were now withdrawing their support. Progressive Islamic leaders had for some time been something of a loyal opposition in Indonesia, at the forefront of peaceful campaigns for political reform. In fact, they had been leading the push for reform not just in the years immediately before Suharto's resignation but for several decades. Some of the voices of dissent were muted so much that they were often inaudible. Other voices, most particularly Abdurrahman Wahid's, had articulated the reformist push loudly and clearly from the beginning of the 1990s when Suharto had turned to his former critics, the radical Islamists, and had tried to buy them off, and sought to outflank and silence moderate progressives from within Islamic civil society at the same time.

In the early 1990s relations between Suharto and Wahid deteriorated substantially when Wahid increasingly criticised the President's initiatives to court the support of radical Islamists. Wahid and others argued that this appeasement of sectarian sentiment would only result in greater sectarianism and would threaten minority communities both inside and outside the Islamic *ummah*. In response to Suharto's sponsorship of the Indonesian Association of Muslim Intellectuals (ICMI), Wahid called upon friends such as Djohan Effendi, Islamic intellectual and speechwriter for Suharto, to put together an alternative forum which they called Forum Demokrasi. Although little more than an elite ginger group the forum was nevertheless the source of great annoyance to Suharto, particularly when Wahid used it as a vehicle to launch attacks on Suharto's appeasement of sectarianism.

Things reached a head in 1994 when Wahid stood for the third time for election as executive chairman of NU for a final five-year term. Suharto did virtually everything he could to block Wahid's re-election. At the time Suharto was at the height of his powers and there was almost no-one either inside or outside government who could consistently stand up to him and get away with it. Wahid proved to be the exception, although he too was finally forced to seek a rapprochement with Suharto in late 1996 in the wake of the violent suppression of Megawati Sukarnoputri's supporters within the Democratic Party of Struggle (PDI-P). Wahid continued to represent the most consistent articulation of reformist dissent against the Suharto regime. Although the rapprochement with Suharto in 1996 and the effective nullification of PDI-P meant that Wahid saw no advantage in leading a campaign against Suharto's Golkar party in the 1997 elections, by the time the Asian economic crisis began to hit Indonesia in the second half of the year, he was once again at the forefront of calls for reform. A near-fatal stroke in January 1998 saw him bedridden and out of action for much of the first half of the year, including the days leading up to Suharto's resignation in May. It was nevertheless hardly surprisingly that no sooner had he partly recovered in June 1998, than he was actively leading preparations for the elections promised for July 1999.

Just as his rapprochement with Suharto in late 1996 proved to be controversial, so too was his initiative in forming a new party, the Partai Kebangkitan Rakyat (PKB—the National Awakening Party), to capture the traditionalist Islamic vote represented by NU. Many saw this as a direct contradiction of the principle of separating religion and politics, which he had previously championed. He argued that it was exactly in practical support of this principle that he had formed the new party. Until this point, he reasoned that traditionalist Muslims had only had the choice of supporting Partai Persatuan Pembangunan (United Development Party), or voting for an entirely secular party.

In creating PKB, he argued, he was giving voice to the aspirations of traditionalist Muslims by providing a vehicle that supported the principles of Pancasila and secular democracy and was critical of Islamist aetiology. His admirers saw in this approach his typically brilliant tactical footwork, combined with a genuine commitment to democratic principles worked out in a practical fashion. His critics, however, saw this as proof of the fact that he was prepared to sacrifice everything to further his political interests. The first group saw him as a consistent, if somewhat eccentric, idealist, whereas the latter saw him as driven by ego and self-interest. The Wahid presidency did little to shift this split in opinion. The very fact that he was prepared to put himself forward as a presidential candidate against Megawati in the October 1999 'Super Parliamentary Elections' of the President was proof to many that Wahid was not only delusional but also entirely self-absorbed. His stroke in January 1998 had robbed him completely of his eyesight, which, although it had deteriorated because of glaucoma, had been good enough for him to read and move around freely before his illness. When he stood for president in October 1999 he was not only so unsteady on his feet because of his stroke that he needed help to walk, but also totally blind.

Even in good health, he represented an unlikely choice for president. As executive chairman of NU for 15 years he had played a transformative role in the organisation's culture and intellectual environment, but his managerial and administrative style had drawn criticism. He seemed a most unlikely and inappropriate choice for Indonesia's first democratically-elected president. Admittedly, Megawati, whom everyone had expected to become president, not least because her party had polled 34% of the Parliamentary votes in the July elections whereas Wahid's party had barely cleared 13%, had no track record of effective leadership and there was no reason to believe she would subtly acquire the interest or the capacity to be an effective hands-on leader. Indeed, in many ways the logical choice for president was BJ Habibie, even though he continued to suffer from his long association with Suharto. Although he had proved a surprisingly effective transitional president, he had many critics. But it was not criticism of his leadership style that sunk his presidential chances. In fact an objective reading of his presidency shows that he performed much better than anyone expected and proved much more reformist than even his close associates might have expected. Rather, it was his sponsorship of a referendum in East Timor, which from Jakarta's point of view went badly wrong, that was the undoing of his presidential bid. Critical here was the fact that he had never had the backing of the military and that in 'giving away' East Timor he compounded his alienation from the military and from powerful elements within his own Golkar party. At the very least, he made it easy for his collegues to move against him and argue that it would be better to have Megawati, or even Wahid, as president rather than Habibie. In the end, it was likely that Megawati's popularity and strong parliamentary support base inclined former supporters of Habibie to rally behind Wahid.

It was not that these people expected Wahid to be an effective president and an acceptable compromise; they calculated that the eccentric Islamic leader, incapacitated by blindness and the effects of his stroke, would be an easy target to control or to replace. It was widely expected that Wahid would continue in his outspoken style and undermine his own credibility, and that it would be easy to conduct a campaign to discredit him. And indeed, so it proved to be. What didn't work out in quite the way many expected, however, was that Wahid refused to be intimidated into giving ground to more powerful interests around him.

Habibie had proven to be an unexpectedly reformist president precisely because he played the role as a non-political actor, as somebody who wasn't constantly calculating his political capital and making rational choices about what he could do. Wahid also achieved what he did by not playing according to the conventional rules. Both transitional presidents refused to recognise the limitations of their political capital and the extent to which these curbed their capacity to push through bold reforms. Both men acted with cavalier disregard for their own political fortunes, preferring instead to do what they believed was needed, regardless of the cost. This proved to be an enormous blessing to Indonesia. Habibie and Wahid were not great presidents–it is easy to build the case that they were deeply flawed–but they were arguably the right sort of presidents to have at a time when the job of being President of Indonesia was impossible.

It is much easier to identify some clear successes during Habibie's presidency than during Wahid's. Habibie pushed through a series of significant reforms. Some of them, such as the moves to decentralise the governing of Indonesia, were somewhat ill-considered and rushed. Nevertheless, it seems clear that it was better for these reforms to have been pushed through imperfectly than not to have been attempted at all. There will continue to be debate about the benefits and costs of decentralisation, but it can, nevertheless, be counted as one of the great achievements of the Habibie presidency. Perhaps even more unexpected was the extent to which Habibie pushed through reforms relating to press freedom and political expression, including insisting on the release of many political prisoners. A cautious conventional politician would probably not have done these things, or have done them only in part, but it proved good for Indonesia that they were done as quickly and as extensively as they were. The referendum in East Timor is perhaps the most contentious aspect of Habibie's presidency, but even that is marked by a genuine desire to follow through on democratic principles and to move Indonesia beyond the problems that bedeviled it during the Suharto years. It seems likely that history will be kind to Habibie. Indeed it does not take too much imagination to conceive of a very different trajectory for the democratisation process, if somebody else, for example, armed forces head General Wiranto, had been made interim president instead of Habibie.

When it comes to assessing the Wahid presidency it is much harder to compile a list of concrete achievements. There is no doubt that Wahid, just as much as Habibie, contributed to the transformation of Indonesian political life in key areas and that, like Habibie, he did so without regard for the political cost and, consequently, acted in a way that was not strictly rational for a professional politician. It can also be argued that the Wahid presidency was a vital period in the nation's transition to democracy and that, if there had been a different interim president at this point, reforms might not have been pushed through to the extent that they were. For example, had Megawati become President in October 1999, she would probably, unlike Wahid, have served her five-year term. It is likely that she would have delivered more stability, but Indonesia would probably not have continued on the course of reform set by Habibie. It is, however, not easy to explain exactly why the nation did continue with Habibie's reforms under Wahid. Whereas Habibie's presidency was marked by a series of legislative reforms and achievements, Wahid's presidency was not.

It would appear that Wahid's greatest contribution as President of Indonesia lay rather more in the transformation of culture and the raising of expectations than in managerial successes and achievements, as was the case during his period of leadership within NU. A careful consideration of the challenges facing Wahid and the choices that he made reveals this aspect of his leadership. It is all too easy to focus on his gaffes, whether they were real or merely the unfair smears of well-funded media campaigns, and his failure to run a stable and conventional presidency that inspired confidence and fostered stability. Criticisms of this kind cannot be avoided and there can be no pretending that Wahid did not fail to do many of the things that were in his power to do and could so easily have boosted confidence in his leadership. At the same time, he gave his opponents opportunity to criticise him because he was far freer and more open with the media than any professional politician would dare to be, and because he spoke frankly on matters about which he was not always fully briefed or which he had not thoroughly considered, in a way that an astute politician would have easily avoided.

There is no denying that the cost of having such an unconventional and unlikely president was often high and that the result was a much less stable and confident government than many in the business and international communities would have liked. Nevertheless, when the various challenges facing him and his responses to them are considered, it becomes clear that, although he lacked Habibie's efficient machinery and methodical approach to management, Wahid continued the course of reform begun by Habibie and added his own elements.

The residual effects of the Asian economic crisis on Indonesia's depressed economy and battered national currency were among the immediate challenges facing Wahid. Expectations of the first democratically-elected president were high, perhaps higher in civil society than in the business sector. The new president was expected to stabilise and strengthen the exchange rate and restore a measure of economic growth that would redress the damage of the previous two years, while at the same time reforming the military and tackling the effects of four decades of authoritarian rule on the civil service and governance. The better informed observers understood that it would take the best part of a decade to start to achieve these things and decades more to complete them. But this did not stop even those who should have known better from lambasting Wahid when he failed to work miracles. It is true that a more conventional style of government with less controversy and greater stability might have helped consolidate economic growth a little more quickly than Wahid's government did, but it is unlikely that anyone could have begun to deliver on all the expectations heaped upon Indonesia's first democratically-elected president. Indeed many in the foreign media at the time acknowledged that being President of Indonesia at the beginning of the 21st century represented one of the world's most difficult political assignments. It was perhaps inevitable that whoever took on the task would end up being widely discredited and criticised and perhaps even, as happened to Wahid, put out of office early by a parliamentary vote of no confidence.

Despite all this negativity, however, a number of things were achieved during Wahid's presidency which were not sufficiently acknowledged at the time and tend to be overlooked subsequently. The first achievement was the President's firm stand against the military. This reformist stance cost him dearly, but arguably achieved lasting success. Had an active or retired military general taken over the interim presidency after Suharto's resignation it is likely that military reform would have taken a very different course. The success of the Habibie presidency laid the foundation for military reform. It was not so much that Habibie himself pushed through many specifically military reform initiatives but that he demonstrated that, in a time of crisis, Indonesia didn't need the military to intervene and take charge. It is partly because of this that some elements of the military took the opportunity afforded by the East Timor referendum to create havoc with their long-term military contacts. Whether this actually helped their position, however, is debatable.

When Wahid became President, one of his clear ambitions was to ensure the gradual reform of the military and to prevent its return to the political stage. Wahid had a longstanding reputation as a campaigner for minority rights and as somebody who was not afraid to speak up on human rights abuse. He had a record of taking on the military. Nevertheless, despite common misconceptions, his approach to dealing with the military and to military reform was reasonably sophisticated and carefully calibrated, even though his personal style implied that everything he did was reckless and spontaneous. In fact, Wahid approached military reform with a greater level of preparedness and down-to-earth, or *Realpolitik*, commonsense than he displayed on almost any other front. He had been working for some time on the Aceh issue, meeting with senior Acehnese religious leaders in Aceh and in Jakarta, and quietly talking at the same time with senior military figures. He entered his presidency with a determination to avoid, as far as possible, an all-out confrontation with the military, preferring to chip away at key issues and work with reformist elements within the military as much as he could.

What changed this approach was the wash-up of the East Timor violence. Although Wahid had long been sympathetic to the cause of the East Timorese he, like most members of the Jakarta elite, fully expected that a referendum in East Timor would result in majority support for remaining within the Republic. This struck him and others as the most sensible option available to the East Timorese. What they did not sufficiently understand was the extent of military brutality during the occupation, particularly before and after the August 1999 referendum. It was not that they had not heard some of the bad stories, but the details of these incidents that reached them were filtered. As President, Wahid had access to certain kinds of information, but this information was much less complete than might have been expected. Certainly the military was not about to tell him things they did not want him to know. And on almost every other front there was a steely resistance to his reformist inclinations within the remaining edifice of the Suharto regime which persisted in the Indonesian civil service, including within the State Secretariat responsible for the running of the presidential palace, who continually undermined Wahid's efforts to get on with the day-to-day business of governing.

By early 2000 Wahid had realised that what had happened in East Timor around the time of the referendum represented abuse that was much worse and more flagrant than he had been informed of or had previously believed. The single key factor in changing his view of these matters, and in consequently hardening his approach to military reform, was the information given to him first-hand over many weeks by his second daughter Yenny. Yenny was constantly by his side, acting as a kind of informal chief of staff–cum–personal assistant, giving assistance that was vital given his blindness and other physical shortcomings and the lack of suitable administrative support. Having become blind recently and suddenly, Wahid was in denial about his blindness and not open to using technology or to learning techniques that would have helped him cope independently. So, rather than using a scanning and dictation machine to read on his own he relied upon assistants like Yenny to read aloud to him and brief him on developing affairs.

An ordinary government minister in most democratic nations would have had a much larger support staff than did the President of Indonesia. This was partly because of his own circumstances, including his blindness, but it was mostly because Suharto had ruled for more than three decades and had shaped the public service into a loyal fiefdom which was completely opposed to submitting to a democratically-elected leader following Suharto's resignation. The Indonesian public service had and continues to have complicated laws relating to promotion and staffing appointments. At face value these appear to be reasonable regulations, but the existing civil service was a creature of the Suharto regime and was accustomed either to direct control by the president or to defining its own path in ways that had been licensed by the president. This meant that, when the first democratically-elected president wished to bring with him his own support staff, it was extremely difficult to do so and was met with active resistance from the civil service and the legislature. Following the inauguration of a new American president, more than 6000 new political appointments are made in Washington DC, giving the incoming president a strong multilayered team of loyal advisers and aides. When Wahid became President he struggled to put together a team of several dozen people and found that, even then, much of his support had to be informal and personal because he could not formally add his staff to the civil service machinery.

Immediately prior to her father's election, Yenny had worked as a journalist for the *Age* in Melbourne and the *Sydney Morning Herald*, and as such she had covered the referendum in East Timor, winning with her team a Walkley Award for reporting on the referendum. Whereas her foreign colleagues were obliged to leave Dili shortly before the referendum and return some time afterwards, she was able to remain there throughout the period, living with some degree of security at a military base. This meant that she witnessed first-hand extraordinary scenes of violence and understood something of the extent of military responsibility for that violence. She relayed her experiences to her father finding him, initially, somewhat resistant to accepting her account of what had happened in Dili. Eventually, however, she convinced him that what happened was very much worse than he had understood from his official briefings. This persuaded him to make an official visit to Dili on 29 February 2000 where he stood on a podium in the centre of the town alongside Xanana Gusmão and apologised to the people of East Timor for the mistakes and misdeeds of his military and his people and promised to build a better future together. This, to say the least, was not received well by many senior military officers.

Taking a conciliatory approach to his dealings with the military, Wahid had appointed General Wiranto to his Cabinet as Co-ordinating Minister for Politics and Security. Once he understood the extent of military-backed militia violence in East Timor at the time of the referendum, he decided that Wiranto, who had commanded troops in East Timor at the time, should be sacked. Wiranto did his best to put his case to the President and briefly appeared to have won, but in the end he was sacked with the face-saving explanation that somebody needed to take responsibility for events in in East Timor. Wiranto had never been close to Wahid nor had he supported him; the sacking turned him into a dangerous, albeit smiling, enemy. From this point on Wahid intervened more directly in military appointments and reforms. He was arguably doing what a democratic president should do, but the military saw it as unjustified meddling and set about finding ways to discredit his administration. Wahid found a strategic ally in General Agus Wirahadikusumah and made him leader of Kostrad, the Strategic Reserves Command of the Indonesian Army (TNI), in March 2000. Agus was to prove an able reformer and assisted with a number of changes within TNI, not least addressing systemic corruption within the Kostrad. Wahid intended to promote him further to make him army chief of staff but gave up when faced with concerted and vigorous resistance to the promotion from senior generals.

In March 2000 Wahid entered into formal negotiations with leaders of the Free Aceh Movement, which led to the signing of a memorandum of understanding in May 2000. The relationship broke down by the beginning of 2001, but arguably was a step along the path towards a negotiated peace in Aceh, which was completed following the tsunami that devastated the province in December 2004. Wahid was also interested in taking a similar approach in Papua. He travelled to Jayapura, the capital of Papua, in late December 1999 and stayed to greet the new year in Indonesia's easternmost city. While he was in Papua he engaged in open talks with Papuan leaders and entertained the possibility of reducing troop numbers in the province if social stability could be guaranteed through communal mechanisms.

Wahid's relations with senior generals reached the point of serious breakdown when, against his express orders, 7,000 would-be *mujahidin* who had signed up with Laskar Jihad were given safe transit from Java to Ambon through Surabaya and issued with military weapons. By this point it was clear that elements of the military were actively campaigning against the President and were doing all that they could to discredit his administration and to boost the argument for military intervention in troubled regions and remind the nation that at times of crisis the TNI was indispensable. Wahid's tougher stand against the military saw senior generals flee to Megawati, a politician they had long admired because she harboured none of the desire for military reform that Wahid had talked about for decades. The experience of the Wahid presidency confirmed in their minds that their interests would be much better served with Megawati as President.

A similar dynamic occurred in political reform. Just as the opening days of the presidency gave the new president the opportunity to seek a negotiated peace with his opponents in the military and make a deal with them to gain a degree of support, so too with the political elites. Wahid could easily have made a deal with power-brokers such as Golkar chairman Akhbar Tanjung but refused, partly out of belligerence and partly as a matter of principle. Throughout the course of his presidency he made a series of poor judgement calls that cost him the goodwill of other parties. For example, he sacked the popular and well-regarded Laksamana Sukadi, one of PDI-P's brightest young leaders from his Cabinet on grounds of alleged corruption, but he damaged his position by failing to produce evidence openly. Many of his battles with the political elite, however, were not merely the product of his erratic style or combative personality but involved concerns about compromising the reform process.

Wahid's critics tirelessly found ways to discredit him and undermine his administration. They beat up scandals, in particular accusing him of wrongful use of funds from a government agency, BULOG, and of handling a donation from the Sultan of Brunei inappropriately. There were certainly irregularities in both of these matters, but, despite the best efforts of his critics, no systemic impropriety was found. In the end, when Wahid was forced to step down as President in July 2000 it was because of a vote of no confidence in the Parliament rather than, as is often assumed, because allegations of corruption were found to be true. Had he been prepared to cut deals with the civilian elite, as he was asked to do with the military elite, he may well have been able to serve out his full term of office.

It is arguable that, despite the high price he paid for not cutting such deals, he had little to show for his principled stand by way of lasting achievements. But this would be an unduly cynical reading of events. If he achieved nothing else, his insistence on reform raised the expectations of the public and the intelligentsia to the extent that subsequent governments were measured against much higher standards than might have otherwise been possible. After his presidency the Indonesian people had new expectations of what democracy might bring and of what could be reasonably demanded of the new leadership.

One of the greatest disappointments in Wahid's performance was his failure to bring convictions against either the former president or members of his family and inner circle. For a while it appeared as if he was making good progress when he appointed a tough-minded reformer as Attorney-General. Sadly he died suddenly in suspicious circumstances; there was no autopsy to determine why he should have had a heart attack when he had no family history or evidence in his personal medical records of heart problems. His death may have been entirely coincidental, but it did seem to put the brakes on the ambitious anti-corruption investigations he had launched. In recent years there has been a return to this kind of tough-minded investigation and it is now commonplace for senior politicians to face corruption investigations and for many to be tried, found guilty and sentenced. This sort of reform was unimaginable before Suharto's resignation; it seems that, to a certain extent, the Wahid presidency, and the Habibie presidency before it, made this possible, if only by raising the expectations of the Indonesian people.

One area in which Wahid, building on the earlier good work of Habibie, made progress was press freedom and general transparency. Although he was often harried by the media, partly because of his tendency to talk too much but also because of concerted, well-funded campaigns, and although he was often frustrated to the point of expressing his desire to see the press more tightly controlled, Wahid remained a constant supporter of press freedom. He refused to take action against members of the media, which Megawati did not shy away from, even when the evidence suggested that he had good reason for doing so.

He spoke articulately and consistently in support of press freedom and consolidated the reforms that Habibie had initiated to the extent that those reforms were not substantially retracted even during the rather listless years of the Megawati presidency. Today Indonesia enjoys a vigorous free press and part of the credit for that must go to the transitional presidencies of Habibie and Wahid. Whereas Suharto was famously taciturn and reluctant to give interviews, much less hold discussions with either the media or the intelligentsia, Wahid was open and engaging. His regular meet-the-press sessions following Friday prayers often caused him grief. Nevertheless, he succeeded in raising expectations of how a democratic president should act and those expectations have borne fruit.

Another major contribution he made as President was to give to the world a sense of Indonesia as a normal democracy. This was particularly poignant, as he was well-known as a respected Muslim cleric. His commitment to openness reinforced the sense that Islam and democracy need not be incompatible. Wahid travelled tirelessly as President seeking to convey to the world a sense of an

Indonesia that had been transformed and was attractive to foreign investment. In terms of encouraging investment he had little to show for his efforts. Indonesia has struggled ever since the 1997 financial crisis to attract direct foreign investment and has found that funds that previously floated in its direction are now directed towards China, India and Vietnam. It would be wrong to blame the failure to attract foreign investors on Wahid alone; it may well have been the case that, had he not reached out to the world, things might have been even worse.

From the beginning of his presidency he made foreign tours a priority, which a more astute, professional and conventional politician might not have done. In November 1999 he visited Indonesia's neighbours before going to Japan, the United States, Kuwait and Jordan. The next month he made a trip to China, a key symbolic and practical move for an Indonesian President. In January he participated in the World Economic Forum at Davos, Switzerland and made a point of visiting Saudi Arabia on his journey home. In February he visited the United Kingdom, France, the Netherlands, Germany and Italy before returning home via India, South Korea, Thailand and Brunei. In April he, rather controversially, attended the Group of 77 summit of developing nations in Cuba visiting South Africa, Mexico and Hong Kong on this trip as well. Although the United States was unhappy about his visit to Cuba, they welcomed him in June, when he also visited Japan, France, Pakistan, Iran and Egypt. Throughout his presidency he talked of making a visit to Indonesia's important neighbour Australia, something that no Indonesian president had done since 1972. Mounting political troubles meant that this visit was delayed until June 2001, towards the end of his presidency. Despite the fact that he was by then something of a lame-duck president, the visit was a great success and reinforced a sense that Indonesia had changed and wanted to reach out to the world. Like most aspects of the Wahid presidency, what was achieved with these trips is more easily recognised in terms of symbolism than substance, but, despite the lack of substance, the symbolism itself was extremely important. Even Megawati, who was not inclined to engage in international affairs, felt the pressure to travel and match her predecessor, as did Susilo Bambang Yudhoyono. These efforts did not by any means completely transform Indonesia's low profile in international affairs, but they did mark the beginning of a change.

Perhaps Wahid's symbolic push for reform was most clearly seen in considerations of the nature of secular democracy in Indonesia and the position of ethnic and religious minorities. Much to the chagrin of his Islamist critics, Wahid took every possible opportunity to outline his vision of a Muslim majority Indonesia that was at ease with secular democracy and that valued religious and cultural diversity. Throughout his public career he gave his support to Indonesia's

Chinese and Christian communities. He took the opportunity of being President to celebrate Chinese New Year openly with community members in Jakarta and Surabaya in February 2000 and again in February 2001, when he made Chinese New Year an optional national holiday. This saw a transformation of public expression of Chinese culture, aided by the official dropping of the ban on the display of Chinese characters and importation of Chinese literature. To those not familiar with Suharto's Indonesia these might seem like small things, but they represented a sea change in official attitudes towards Indonesia's Chinese minority. It by no means removed all of their problems, but it did mark an important shift towards openly recognising their contributions to Indonesian society and towards allowing them freedom to express their cultural identity. Similarly, Christian and other minority religious communities welcomed the President's championing of their freedom of religion and his recognition of the value of their contribution to the Republic.

After a short presidency that ended in an ignominious fashion, it might be thought that he achieved little. His enduring contributions seemed largely symbolic in nature and, during the subsequent Megawati presidency, it appeared as if most important reforms were being wound back, as progress towards press freedom, reform of the military and peace negotiations in Aceh and Papua was reversed. In the longer term, however, it can be seen that the Habibie and Wahid presidencies laid the groundwork for the open democracy now evident in Indonesia. Once basic reforms had been put through and the expectations of the general public and the elite transformed, the way was open for substantial democratisation in a way that would have been impossible if Indonesia's first and second post-Suharto presidents in that key transitional period had been conventional politicians more concerned with preserving their political capital. In conclusion it should be noted that both Habibie and Wahid were identified as representing Muslim interests in Indonesia and yet both proved to be firm supporters of secular liberal democracy. The fact that while Wahid, who had trained as an *alim*, a religious cleric, and was well regarded within that sphere should become such a liberal president, for all his failings, was a matter of great significance. Although it may not have been clear at the time, history will record that, in many different ways, Indonesia got lucky with these transitional presidents, whose reformist approaches enabled a democratic transition that was not supposed to fly to rise off the ground and move forward.

chapter four

Megawati and the legacy of Sukarno

Angus McIntyre

As President of Indonesia between 1945 and 1967, Sukarno sought to realise particular versions of government and the nation state. It goes without saying that he intended his achievements in these two areas to outlast him; to constitute, therefore, his legacy to the Indonesian people. But a legacy may also mean, in addition to something deliberately handed down by a predecessor to subsequent generations, an unintended effect or consequence of an act or process. In this second sense, Sukarno's legacy included events and upheavals which he had not even imagined, let alone intended, but to which he nevertheless contributed.

His daughter, Megawati, who assumed the presidency in 2001, was devoted to her father's memory and very much preoccupied with his legacy, engaging its components with varying degrees of flexibility and inventiveness. If she anxiously and narrowly defended her father's conception of the nation state, she strove to the limits of her understanding and ability to reconcile his preferred form of government with the democratic tendencies of her own time. Thus she bestowed a degree of nationalist legitimacy on Indonesia's emerging presidential democracy.

Sukarno's legacy

The nation state

From the late 1920s, Sukarno was one of a number of so-called 'secular nationalists'[1] who conceived of the Indonesian people in territorial terms, as simply the indigenous inhabitants of the Netherlands Indies. This seemingly unremarkable formulation signified an Indonesian nationalism that was anticolonial and emancipatory on the one hand and, given the extraordinary diversity of these inhabitants, multicultural or civic on the other.

The civic quality of this nationalism was strengthened by Sukarno's success in providing Muslims and Christians with a common religious basis for allegiance to the new Republic. In an address before the Japanese-sponsored Investigating

Committee for the Preparation of Indonesian Independence (Badan Penyelidik Usaha Persiapan Kemerdekaan Indonesia) on 1 June 1945, he advanced five principles—his speech was subsequently entitled *Lahirnya Panca Sila* (The Birth of the Five Principles)—to underpin the new Republic, one of which stated that 'belief in the one God' should form the basis of a 'Theistic State'. Subsequently, this principle, elevated from last to first position, was incorporated, along with the other four, into the preamble of the 1945 Constitution. This nationalism worked well at first, although it must be conceded that significant exceptions to this proposition were to be found in the separatist revolts in the South Moluccas (1950) and Aceh (1953) and in the Darul Islam insurgency (1949–62), the embers of which continue to glow.

However, at the very time that Sukarno spelled out his principle of the state based on a 'belief in the one God', he also proved receptive to the idea, advanced by Mohammed Yamin, one of his colleagues on the Investigating Committee, of an Indonesian Fatherland extending beyond the boundaries of the Netherlands Indies. It was left to an officer in the Imperial Japanese Army to save the honour of Indonesia's anti-colonial and civic nationalism, for it was only at the insistence of Marshal Terauchi, the Commander-in-Chief for Southeast Asia, that Sukarno subsequently settled for the territory of the former Netherlands Indies.

In subsequent years, President Sukarno, as he became on 18 August 1945, again placed his country's nationalism under great strain by continuing to insist, in an uncompromising manner, that the remote, isolated and very different West New Guinea was an integral part of Indonesia on the grounds that it too had been included within this colonial territory. The unsurprising emergence there of a separatist movement once Sukarno and his government took over from the Dutch in 1963 challenged Indonesian nationalism at its anti-colonial core, and the patronising and racist attitudes of the people of Western Indonesia towards their 'stone-age' brothers and sisters corroded its civic quality (Liddle 1997:282, *passim*).

It was not only the manner of Sukarno's stance on West New Guinea that posed a challenge to the attributes of Indonesia's nationalism. Its civic quality was also called into question by anti-Chinese sentiment within the country. Anthony Reid has written in this regard of Indonesia's and the Philippines' 'nationalisms of citizenship' being 'ambivalent or negative about including Chinese cultures among the ethnic diversity in which they rejoice', although he added that 'their inherent pluralism provides a framework within which it could be done' (Reid 1997:57). This was not a problem of Sukarno's making; he himself did not seem to share this ambivalence or negativity, although he was not above trying to provoke anti-Chinese riots in Singapore and the Malay Peninsula during Konfrontasi (see Mackie 1974:259).

If Sukarno appeared free of ethnic prejudice and, unlike his successor, did not resort to making a scapegoat of the Chinese minority within Indonesia, he nevertheless came—in the late Guided Democracy years—to wield political categories with a certain exclusionary zeal. His various political formulas and slogans became shibboleths which he used to distinguish between revolutionaries and counter-revolutionaries, loyalists and traitors, and true and false Indonesians. This last distinction is particularly telling, and shows that in his later years, Sukarno retreated from his earlier civic nationalism into something much more divisive—not ethnic nationalism, but what might be called its political equivalent.

Government

A nationality defined in territorial terms was often considered the most promising basis on which to realise the old assumption that liberty for the individual and for the nation were intrinsically linked (Namier 1962:46). Indonesian nationality was so defined, but Sukarno was adamant that the sovereignty of the people did not imply the sovereignty of individuals, and insisted, therefore, 'that citizens' rights had no place in Indonesia' (Bourchier 1996:92 *passim*). The 1945 Constitution, of which he was an author, reflected this authoritarian perspective. Its first article proclaimed the Indonesian state to be a unitary one, thereby defying the democratic preference for federal arrangements in the government of vast territories. It had nothing to say about the method of selection of the People's Consultative Assembly (Majelis Permusyawaratan Rakyat), in which the sovereignty of the people supposedly resided, nor even of the People's Representative Council (Dewan Perwakilan Rakyat), and it contained neither an assertion of judicial independence nor a robust defence of individual rights.

A presidential dictatorship, to use AK Pringgodigdo's description (Pringgodigdo 1957:5–6), based on this constitution and its transitional provisions came into being on 18 August 1945. One of its components, apparently established on Sukarno's initiative (Bourchier 1996:102), was a *staatspartij* intended to mobilise the population behind the national leadership (Anderson 1972:95). However, this organisation and the government of which it was a part were soon swept aside by a wave of democratic sentiment among the country's citizens. It was not until the second cabinet of Prime Minister Ali Sastroamidjojo (1956–57), the first to be drawn from the parliament elected in 1955, proved unable to deal with the challenge posed by regional disaffection and unrest within the army and civilian population that Sukarno gained another opportunity to give expression to his authoritarian political inclinations.

In October 1956 Sukarno argued that Indonesia's political parties should be buried, on the grounds that they were having an injurious effect on the unity and wellbeing of the nation. But, in the face of strong opposition from the parties themselves, he dropped the idea. Then, in February 1957, he suggested the formation of a cabinet of mutual co-operation (*gotong royong*) in which the representatives of all major parties, including the Communist Party (Partai Komunis Indonesia (PKI)) would sit. His justification that it was not practical to exclude from the process of government a group that attracted six million votes in recent elections was anathema to the regional military commanders and failed to persuade the leaders of the other major political parties. In the midst of this uncertainty, the Army Chief of Staff, General Nasution, and President Sukarno devised a drastic response to the regional challenge. Under its terms, Ali Sastroamidjojo returned his cabinet's mandate to the President on 14 March and 30 minutes later he proclaimed a state of war and siege for the whole country.

A year later Nasution directed an effective military operation against the regionalists' newly- proclaimed Revolutionary Government of the Republic of Indonesia (Pemerintah Revolusioner Republic Indonesia). Thereafter, Sukarno, with the support and encouragement of Nasution, embarked on the road to authoritarian government. On 5 July 1959 he issued a presidential decree which dissolved the Constituent Assembly—elected together with the parliament in 1955—abrogated the Constitution of 1950, and re-enacted the 1945 Constitution. And far from the rebellions recommending to Sukarno the value of Law 1/1957 passed by the second Ali Cabinet to enlarge the scope of local government, the President issued a decree in September 1959 which vitiated its contents. Then, in March 1960, he dissolved the elected parliament after it threatened to reject the government's budget, and endorsed the same budget by decree. In August he banned the small Socialist Party and the modernist Islamic political party, Masjumi, on the grounds of their involvement in the regional rebellion, even though Masjumi had received almost eight million votes in the parliamentary elections of 1955.

If regional autonomy and democracy were the first casualties of Sukarno's emerging authoritarianism, the rule of law was the second. In February 1960, he made the chairman of the Supreme Court, Wirjono Prodjodikoro, a cabinet member. Six months later, he denounced the principle of the separation of powers in a speech to the Interim People's Consultative Assembly. Laws 19/1964 and 13/1965 gave direct expression to the President's views by allowing government involvement in the course of justice and explicitly ending judicial autonomy. The official explanation to Law 13/1965 states:

> This law...realises the idea that the separation of powers doctrine (Trias Politika) no longer applies in Indonesian society. The concept that judges shall be impartial, independent from any external interference, can no longer be upheld and has been buried (Pompe 2005:52).

In 1960 he also began espousing his Nasionalis-Agama-Komunis doctrine that asserted the legitimate existence of a communist stream in Indonesian society, of which the PKI was the representative, together with religious and nationalist streams.

Sukarno first encountered Marxism in his high school years. Thereafter, it permeated his thinking, shaped his view of history and gave form to his aspirations for an independent Indonesia. In 1959, a few months after the return (as it was called) to the 1945 Constitution, he had socialism declared an official objective of the Indonesian nation and it was not long before he most fancifully transformed this goal into reality. In April 1965, the year in which continuing budget deficits caused inflation to reach an annual rate of 600% (Mackie 1974:88–90), Sukarno stated that Indonesia was entering the stage of Sosialisme Indonesia (Hauswedell 1973:127–28, 128n73).

The President assembled his so-called 'Guided Democracy' in difficult and complex circumstances in which he was obliged to share power with the military under General Nasution. Nevertheless, one may discern key elements within it that were central to his thinking and practice over a lengthy period and which, it seems safe to assume, he regarded as having enduring value. They were authoritarian government based on the 1945 Constitution in which the judiciary would be subordinate to the executive, a unitary state allowing only very limited scope for regional government, and the bringing into being of socialism in Indonesia.

An unimagined massacre

These key elements, then, may be viewed as Sukarno's legacy in the area of government. The remaining aspect includes the event that he had not intended but contributed to nevertheless—namely, the massacre of PKI members in 1965. There is a debate as to what Sukarno's intentions were in the late Guided Democracy years, beyond his wish that Indonesia should embrace socialism—a wish so strong that in September 1965 he twice repeated his fanciful claim of the previous April that Indonesia was already entering the stage of Sosialisme Indonesia (Hauswedell 1973:127–28, 128n73). He appeared determined to integrate the PKI into Guided Democracy, despite the tension that existed between it and anti-communist groups, including the Army—a tension made even worse by a political environment shaped by frantic political mobilisation, soaring inflation and serious food shortages. And his persisting with such efforts in 1964–5, amidst the violence stirred up in the villages of Central and East Java by the PKI's attempt to implement the Land Reform Law of 1960, seemed most reckless.

In the end we are left with a paradox caused by the personal style of rule of President-for-life Sukarno, as he was designated by the Interim People's Consultative Assembly in 1963. On the one hand, his bringing forward of the PKI exacerbated tensions within society; on the other, it was only his presence that prevented the outbreak of direct conflict between the rival parties. Consequently, an expectation took hold within the political elite that Guided Democracy, and the strained political accommodation on which it was built, could not survive Sukarno's death.

As it turned out, it was not his death but a fearful anticipation of it that set in motion a chain of events that brought his presidency and Guided Democracy to an end. As a result of a gloomy prognosis regarding the President's health, occasioned by his falling ill on 4 August 1965, the leader of the PKI, DN Aidit, decided to anticipate the expected attack on the party by the army.[2] The consequences that flowed from this decision were appalling—the killing of almost the entire general staff of the army by a communist-led 'movement' and the mass murder of PKI members and sympathisers at the hands of the surviving generals and their civilian accomplices.

Sukarno was appalled: 'Stop, stop, stop, stop, Brothers and Sisters! Stop, don't go on like this!', he called out at the time (Sukarno 1965:30). Nevertheless, these events, too, constitute part of Sukarno's legacy, making it a most complex matter that would exercise the minds and feelings of subsequent generations of Indonesians, including, of course, his eldest daughter, Megawati.

Megawati

Government

There can be no doubt that authoritarian government was one part of Sukarno's legacy. Yet Megawati, to judge by her exhortation of 23 June 1996—'Remember that what we are fighting for now is defending the sovereignty that is in the hands of the people and to redress the democracy given to us under the 1945 constitution'—and her statement from late September of the same year that 'I am making a serious effort...to remind people again that this state was established as a law state', appeared to regard her father as a democrat and a proponent of the rule of law on the strength of his role as one of the authors of the 1945 Constitution.

Perhaps she had taken at face value the official explication of the 1945 Constitution that proclaimed Indonesia to be a 'state which is based on Law (Rechtsstaat)'. Also, she was no doubt familiar with her father's frequent assertions of love for the people and his no less frequent claims to be uniquely able to give voice to their aspirations. It is very possible that she misconstrued this populist strand in his thinking as a democratic one.[3]

Certainly, she frequently asserted that the arbitrary and tyrannical nature of the New Order government derived from Suharto's deviations from the 1945 Constitution, not from the Constitution itself. In a speech on 28 September 1998, she stated that the centralist policies of the Suharto government were one such example and implied that substantial regional autonomy could, in fact, be implemented within the framework of the unitary state as provided for in Article 1 of the 1945 Constitution. She also endorsed the contents of Article 28—perhaps not realising that it had only been introduced into the Constitution over her father's objections—by saying that 'the right to associate and express opinions has to be guaranteed by law' (Sambutan 1998).

On the other hand, Megawati subsequently became aware of her father's opposition to Montesquieu's liberal constitutionalism based on 'the separation of the legislative, executive and judicial powers' (Sabine 1938:558), and, presumably, of the corresponding failure of the 1945 Constitution to provide for such a separation. We may observe her in March 1999, struggling to reconcile this opposition with her own dawning recognition that the separation of powers was an essential foundation of the rule of law.

> Although Indonesia does not adhere to Montesquieu's Trias Politika system, the PDI [Partai Demokrasi Indonesia]...still holds strongly to the position that there must be a clear and transparent division between the legislative, judicial and executive powers and that this must be applied to our future political system. This division is necessary to prevent the intervention of the executive in the legislative and even judicial branches, as has been the case so far (Megawati 1999).

Similarly, it seems safe to assume that Megawati was familiar not only with Article 33 of the 1945 Constitution which provided for an economy 'based upon the principles of the family system', and required both natural resources and vital sectors of production to 'be controlled by the state', but also with her father's espousal of socialism and its formal establishment as a goal of the state in 1959. Nevertheless, she departed from this orthodoxy in her speech of 28 September 1998, in which she spoke in favour of a market economy, although not an unfettered one: 'Via a democratic political system, the people have the sovereignty to manage the market economy so that besides growth, national economic development also brings about justice and an even distribution of wealth' (Sambutan 1998).

Thus, we may observe Megawati, between 1996 and 1999, acquire a more accurate sense of the true nature of the 1945 Constitution and knowingly depart from her father's legacy by supporting a separation of powers and a market economy. But it is an open question whether she knew of her father's hostility to regional autonomy, manifested in his vitiation of Law 1/1957, when she argued that such autonomy could be reconciled with Article 1 of the 1945 Constitution. It is important not to overstate her support for such autonomy. Evidently, she was somewhat taken aback by the far-reaching nature of Laws 22 and 25 on the decentralisation of government proposed by the Habibie Government and passed by the parliament in 1999.

President Suharto's exclusion of Megawati from the parliament elected in 1997 placed her in a paradoxical position. She was unable to play any meaningful part in the democratic reforms introduced by President Habibie in 1998 and 1999, but, enjoying very widespread popular support as a result of her strong stance against Suharto in previous years, she turned out to be one of their chief beneficiaries. Her political party won a plurality of votes in the 1999 parliamentary elections—the first free national elections held in Indonesia since 1955—and she was elected Vice-President in 1999 and President in 2001.

In these various capacities she played an important role, both in the implementation by the executive of reform legislation, especially Laws 22 and 25 of 1999, and in the amending of the 1945 Constitution by the People's Consultative Assembly. As Vice-President and then President, and as leader of the largest party in the legislature from 1999 to 2004, she was in a position to obstruct this rewriting of the Constitution and, on one occasion, the military actually invited her to do so. Two days before the opening of the Assembly session in August 2002, at which the exclusion of military members from both of its houses was to be considered, General Endriartono Sutarto, the Commander of the military (Tentara Nasional Indonesia (TNI)), claimed that the TNI would support her if she emulated her father by reintroducing the original 1945 Constitution by decree. She refused this invitation to trump tragedy with farce. No doubt, she was reassured by the broad agreement that emerged in the Assembly to leave the Preamble untouched and to preserve Article 1 which provided for a unitary state. It seems that, beyond those two areas, 'she never questioned the assembly's right to amend the constitution or her responsibility to implement its decisions', even though she was opposed to some of its measures (Kim, Liddle & Said 2006:259). Consequently, she did not oppose members of her party voting for the four amendments, thereby ensuring their comparatively smooth passage through the People's Consultative Assembly.

Megawati's hesitant departures from her father's political legacy, as recorded above, were mild compared to her allowing this fundamental transformation of the 1945 Constitution to take place. It is true that she probably saw an opportunity to benefit from some of the amendments, for example, the one providing for the direct election of the President, but it is also true that others troubled her, such as the one that wrote into the Constitution the general principles and core details of Laws 22/1999 and 25/1999. Nevertheless, she allowed the amendments to stand. (In the last months of her presidency she did preside over the passing of Laws 32 and 33/2004 which reduced somewhat the powers given to regional and municipal heads and parliaments under the previous legislation.) (Nordholt & van Klinken 2007:14–15). In so doing, she facilitated a process whereby Indonesia's emerging presidential democracy, and the amended 1945 Constitution that underpinned it, acquired a nationalist legitimacy on account of their derivation from the original 1945 Constitution, one of whose authors was Sukarno, the first President and a founding father of the Republic of Indonesia.

The massacre of 1965

We have seen what Megawati made of her father's political legacy, especially as it was embodied in the 1945 Constitution. But what did she make of its other aspect—the mass killings of PKI members in late 1965? Of course, she may not have seen that event as a consequence of Sukarno's policies and personal style of rule, but she certainly seemed alert to the shortcomings of the latter. In a speech on 10 January 1998, she said: 'To grant...[Suharto] a term of office as president in excess of thirty years amounts to an effort to make him...president for life. The Indonesian nation must not make this mistake for a second time' (Pidato 1998). Also, she noted the prevalence of fear in the late Suharto years and its debilitating consequences for the citizenry at large: 'The feeling of fear is everywhere in the territory of the...Republic of Indonesia, and its presence does not mature but rather stunts the autonomy of the people' (*Kompas* 1995). She did not comment on its origins, but a remark she made to Edward Aspinall suggests she may well have had in mind the 1965 killings, if not of PKI members then of National Party ones. She said to him that 'after joining the...[PDI] in the 1980s, she had always viewed her main task as 'breaking down the old trauma' [the legacy of 1965] in the party's mass support base' (Aspinall 2005:165).[4]

Finally, one wonders whether Megawati's memories of 1965 are partly responsible for the tentative nature of her populism. Both father and daughter were populists, but Sukarno, who endeavoured to mobilise the population behind leftist goals, is best understood as a radical one, whereas Megawati, who appeared wary of the urban poor and could not envisage a relationship with the people to which the military was not also party, adhered to a conservative version of populism.

The nation state

Megawati's flexibility in facilitating the adaptation of Sukarno's authoritarian political legacy to the changed circumstances of her time largely deserted her when she contemplated his version of the Indonesian nation state. In its original formulation, it was territorial in conception and, given that it aimed to supplant Dutch rule over a diverse population, anti-colonial and civic in orientation. Sukarno's refusal to accept the democratic implications of this formulation, as noted above, makes one hesitate to characterise it as emancipatory as well.

Even with this qualification in mind, one may regard this view of the Indonesian nation as comparatively benign, as one that embraces differences and, therefore, as a legacy from which the Indonesian people were likely to benefit. They might have done so, had it not been for the fact that Sukarno immensely complicated matters, less by his brief flirtation with the ethnically-coloured idea of an Indonesian Fatherland than by his extreme application of the territorial principle of Indonesian nationalism to a remote corner of the Netherlands Indies so different as to call into question its anti-colonial and civic qualities. It does not seem to have occurred to Sukarno that a separatist movement might emerge in West New Guinea and challenge the rationale of the Indonesian nation at its weakest point. With the stakes as high as this, no Indonesian government, least of all a democratic one, could possibly grant the separatists their wish. Nevertheless, scope remained for an Indonesian government to respond imaginatively to the grievances of the Papuans, short of granting them independence. This Megawati proved unable to do, weighed down as she was by her loyalty to, and sense of anxious responsibility for, her father's conception of the Indonesian nation state.

In December 1999, two months after becoming Vice-President, Megawati repeated her father's claim that 'without Irian, Indonesia is not complete' (*Suara Pembaruan* 1999). Thereafter, she adopted a firm line against Papuan nationalists. In September 2000, she attended a celebration in Port Moresby marking the 25th anniversary of Papua New Guinea. On her return to Jakarta, she stopped off in Irian where she turned a stony face to Papuan aspirations. 'It is sad', she said, 'that after all this pain and struggle to be part of Indonesia then you emotionally declare your independence'. She added that they should learn from 'the East Timor experience': 'Look at what is happening now in East Timor. One year after they decided to separate from their brothers and sisters, they are still facing several internal problems' (*Jakarta Post* 2000). With sentiments such as these, it is not surprising, perhaps, that she helped push Abdurrahman Wahid's government towards a far more repressive approach in Irian Jaya from November 2000 (Chauvel 2000).

There was another aspect of government policy towards Irian Jaya, dictated by the People's Consultative Assembly. At its session of October 1999, the Assembly, hoping to draw the sting of the separatist movement in Irian, had obliged Wahid's administration to grant special autonomy to the province. In August 2000, it recommended to both the government and the parliament that the appropriate legislation be passed before 1 May 2001 (Ketetapan 2000:37; NDIIA 2000).

This deadline was not met; nevertheless, President Megawati signed the special autonomy bill for Papua (as the province was called in this legislation) on 23 October 2001. It was a substantial law, but the likelihood of it gaining acceptance among the people at whom it was directed was severely limited because of continuing military repression. As stated above, Megawati had, in November 2000, supported a hardening of the military response to independence activists in the province. The arrests, tortures and murders over the following year to which this hardened military response gave rise proved inhospitable soil for the new law to take root in. As one scholar commented: '...it is difficult to imagine how Special Autonomy can be successfully "socialised" and accepted by broad sections of the society in political circumstances of great tension, uncertainty and fear created by the security forces' (Chauvel 2003:43; *Kompas* 2001a).

The law's prospects of acceptance were only made worse when the Papuan leader, Theys Eluay, who 'personified more than any other...the belief that Papuan aspirations could be achieved by non-violent means' (Chauvel 2003:40) was found murdered outside Jayapura on 11 November. He had dined the previous night at the local headquarters of the Special Forces, and Papuans immediately suspected them of being responsible. Subsequently, members of this military unit were charged with the killing; in April 2003, six were convicted and sentenced to prison terms ranging from only two years to three years and six months (*Kompas* 2001b; HRW 2001; 2002; *Sinar Harapan* 2003). The thuggish and simplistic response to these sentences by the Army Chief of Staff, General Ryamizard Ryacudu, offers some insight into the military's talent for exacerbating separatist sentiment. He said:

> I don't know. People say they were wrong and broke the law; okay, we are a law state and they have to be sentenced. But for me they are heroes because they murdered a man who was a rebel, the leader of rebels (*Sinar Harapan* 2003).

It might be protested that President Megawati's confidence in the military surely did not extend to this particular general, and yet such evidence as there is suggests that he was her preferred candidate for the position of Chief of Staff of the Armed Services, in which he was installed in June 2002 (*Suara Merdeka* 2002; *Tempo Interaktif* 2002).

Despite the abovementioned complications, the Special Autonomy Law for Papua offered some hope of reconciling Papuan nationalists to the Republic of Indonesia. However, Megawati and like-minded figures in the military and the Ministry of Interior did not see matters this way. They feared that special autonomy for Papua would lead to its independence (Chauvel & Bhakti 2004:52). Consequently, Megawati issued a presidential instruction (Inpres 1/2003) 'to accelerate the implementation of Law 45/1999' (Chauvel & Bhakti 2004:37). This law was a product of the Habibie presidency, and contained his divisive and blocking response to Papuan demands for independence. Whereas the Special Autonomy Law of 2001 envisaged the single province of Papua, Law 45/1999, which had not been revoked and to which President Megawati now resorted, created the three provinces of Papua, West Irian Jaya and Central Irian Jaya (Chauvel & Bhakti 2004:37). It is a measure of the degradation of Indonesia's anti-colonial nationalism, caused by Sukarno's wilful stance regarding the incorporation of West New Guinea, that Megawati's partitioning of the province of Papua proved reminiscent of the actions of the last Dutch ruler, Lieutenant Governor General HJ van Mook, in creating federal states in order to undermine the standing of the nascent Republic of Indonesia.[5]

Conclusion

It is common to think of Sukarno in grand terms and to relegate his eldest daughter, Megawati, who, in part, owes her prominence to him, to the ranks of the mere epigones. Sukarno's high standing was not undeserved; chief among his accomplishments was the authorship of the principle that the Indonesian state would be based on belief in the one true God. But the leader who built with one hand by offering his Muslim and Christian compatriots this basis for co-existence and co-operation within the one nation, destroyed with the other by subordinating the judiciary to the executive and by adopting an intransigent position regarding the incorporation of West New Guinea into the Republic of Indonesia, thereby compromising the anti-colonial and civic qualities of Indonesian nationalism.

It fell to President Sukarno's comparatively undistinguished daughter to salvage what she could of this deeply flawed legacy. She made no headway in the area of the nation state, where her father had been rash enough to make Papua the keystone in the arch of the Indonesian nation. With the matter posed in this make-or-break fashion, it is perhaps not surprising that an anxious Megawati repudiated special autonomy and used a combination of force and divide-and-rule tactics in order to curb Papuan disaffection. In the area of government, however, she was able to assist in the organic transformation of

Sukarno's presidential dictatorship into a presidential democracy. In so doing, she provided the presidential democracy with a nationalist pedigree reaching back to the Constitution, proclaimed one day after the Declaration of Independence, as well as to one of its authors, her father, the first President of the Republic of Indonesia.

Notes

1 Acknowledgment: The argument of this paper owes a great deal to a number of discussions I have had in recent years with Greg Fealy and Richard Chauvel. The expression is Harry Benda's (1958:79, *passim*).

2 See also John Roosa (2006:145): 'The possibility of Sukarno's death in early August [1965] might have provoked Aidit's initial determination to prepare for a military action...but it could not have sustained that determination through late September' as the President appeared to quickly recover his health.

3 I am grateful to the late Herb Feith for this suggestion.

4 The PDI was a lineal descendant of the pro-Sukarno Indonesian National Party (Partai Nasional Indonesia) formed in early 1946. Some of its members were also killed in the anti-communist massacre of 1965; others actually participated in this killing.

5 I am indebted to Richard Chauvel and Ikrar Nusa Bhakti for this comparison (see Chauvel & Bhakti 2004:40).

chapter five

The bearable lightness of democracy

Ariel Heryanto

Now that Indonesia is entering the second decade of the post-New Order era, under the Susilo Bambang Yudhoyono government (2004–09), Indonesians and analysts of Indonesia should have a better sense of what democracy might mean and entail than they had in 1998. Analysts may differ on the question of whether or not contemporary Indonesia is a democracy and on what basis this term can be defined. Rather than performing another round of conceptual debates on what constitutes a democracy in the abstract, this chapter proceeds with the *a priori* assumption that Indonesia *is* a democracy[1] in order to offer two paradoxical observations. First, in contrast to the generally pessimistic view among Indonesians and their observers alike, I wish to propose that Indonesia is more liberated and democratic than has been generally acknowledged.[2] Second, in what may seem contradictory to the first point, I wish to argue that Indonesia's liberalisation and democratisation does not necessarily mean that all is or will be good. This argument will be presented in a section below in response to the widespread and uncritical valorisation of democracy in academic and non-academic analyses of contemporary Indonesia.

Because I have been an academic and have grown up under the heavy weight of the New Order authoritarian government, I see Indonesia as having achieved more than is generally recognised by Indonesians and foreigners alike. Who should be credited with this achievement is a different question and one that can only be partially answered in this chapter. Admittedly, today's Indonesia is not quite what many were expecting during the final years of the New Order period. Indeed, some of the serious problems from the New Order era have persisted. In some areas, such as money politics, corruption and the poor functioning of the justice system, these problems appear to have become even worse. But it is a serious mistake to consider the two periods (before and after 1998) as two disconnected histories and to judge which is better. Many of the problems in Indonesia today are the direct and indirect consequences of what happened before the last decade.

The New Order and the governments since its decline have operated under significantly different circumstances. While each of these governments started in unfavourable moments (the aftermath of political and economic crises), the New Order enjoyed a great amount of material, military and diplomatic support from the world's major advocates of liberal democracy as part of their strategic moves against the Communist/Socialist bloc during the Cold War. The New Order government brutally eliminated nearly all of the key figures and institutions of its predecessor and fiercely suppressed much of the nation in order to clear the ground and launch its own militaristic development projects during the Cold War.

In contrast, successive post-New Order governments have tried to rebuild Indonesia in a democratic fashion and have done so with much less assistance from the international community. The democratic rebuilding of Indonesia has proved to be more daunting than it first appeared. This is largely a result of the interference from many elements of the New Order elite that survived the 1998 reform movement and have since managed to hijack the outcomes of the reform. Because of the damage done by New Order elites before and after 1998, Indonesians in post-New Order period have had to pay a great price to rebuild the nation. A comparison of the period of the New Order and what has followed must take these historical factors into consideration. Unfortunately, this has proved to be a difficult task for more than a few observers. In fact, many seem to have ignored this problem. Nothing has illustrated this problem more vividly than the mass media coverage of Suharto's critical illness and his death on 27 January 2008. The forgetting of the New Order's state terrorism (Heryanto 2006) and the continued manufacturing of a glorified history of the New Order period are sources of the sense of distress, disillusionment and apathy that can be seen currently among many Indonesians. This malaise is also felt amongst those formerly active in supporting the 1998 reform movement. Another source of this sense of distress, disillusionment and apathy has to do with the myth of democracy as produced and reproduced by analysts of Indonesia. The rest of the chapter will focus on these distinct but interrelated problems.

Demoralisation in democracy and the freedom to express it

Failure to understand the important historical connectedness between Indonesia before and after 1998 has led more than a few to nostalgia for the orderliness of the New Order under Suharto. One recent opinion column in *The Jakarta Post* is entitled 'Why Indonesian people are losing interest in democracy?' (Harijanto 2008). A pessimistic view was more pronounced in the early 2000s. In their longing for a strong ruler, some people chose to remember the past selectively. That is, they emphasised the supposed political stability of the era and the economic growth, ignoring how these were achieved and their costs. They lamented the apparent rise of crime and violence, the stalled economy, all of which they blamed on the rise of Indonesian liberalisation, reform or democratisation.[3]

When Susilo Bambang Yudhoyono—a New Order general—won the presidential elections in 2004, many believed it was a popular expression of disappointment with the disorder since the fall of Suharto and desperation for a return to firm leader with a military background. Working next to the President is an assertive Vice-President, Jusuf Kalla, a New Order tycoon and a top leader of the New Order political machinery, Golkar. The former general has not been a firm and strong leader at all. In fact, he has been considered disappointingly indecisive and slow on too many important issues. These include the impasse with the investigation into the murder of Munir, the aborted establishment of the Commission for Truth and Reconciliation, and the mishandling of the Sidoarjo mudflow. Kalla, on the other hand, has been noted to be remarkably assertive, but often for the wrong reasons. This has raised more worries than assurance among Indonesian reformists and pro-democracy supporters.

The current government can claim little credit for whatever progress has been made in developing Indonesia. There are many problems for which this government must take partial or full responsibility. However, notwithstanding these shortcomings, it is highly contentious to suggest that Indonesia's past, under the New Order, was a better time than what has unfolded since the downfall of the New Order. It is true that Indonesia today is indeed full of problems, but, to say the least, so was Indonesia under the New Order. There is one significant difference though; during the New Order there was no freedom at all to acknowledge and openly discuss the problems that existed.

Today, politics in Indonesia has become noisy, tiring, time-consuming and hopelessly boring. But, so is politics in most other liberal democracies. If politics in some of the world's oldest democracies has lately become occasionally more interesting, this may have something to do with the fact that these countries have become less democratic and more authoritarian, especially after the 11 September 2001 attack in the US.

Notwithstanding the general economic and political performance of the state and private sections that fall short of the naïve and ambitious expectations of the pre-1998 reform movement, Indonesians have enjoyed freedom of expression at a level comparable with most liberal democracies, and perhaps even higher than is found in some of them. The following account illustrates this point. I will juxtapose my account with new and old problems in this area, which should serve as useful counters to my largely positive narrative.

One of the most positive trends since the fall of the New Order has been the strengthening of freedom of expression. While many aspects of this new freedom have been noted by observers, its scale and significance may not be fully recognised and appreciated. We have seen the spectacular growth of the media industry in Indonesia. During the economic crisis a decade ago, when unemployment soared, the mass media was the only industry that recruited more employees. Some companies even doubled their revenue during this period (Hill 2007:10). With the removal of repressive state agencies and policies in 1999, the mass media has become an even more robust institution.[4]

In 1999 President Abdurrahman Wahid closed down the Department of Information—the main propaganda and censorship instrument of the New Order. In the following year, the number of licensed print media publications jumped from 289 to around 1,600. Fewer than half of these publications would survive, however, for reasons that were mainly financial and managerial. The number of private-run television networks has now more than doubled since the end of the New Order era. More than 50 local television stations have spread out across the archipelago, some in ethnic languages; nationwide networks include programs in English and Mandarin.

Another development that demonstrates the remarkable progress of media liberalisation is the new legislation that guarantees the constitutional freedom of media expression. Press Law No. 40/1999 and Broadcasting Law No. 32/2002 are the result of hard-won legal achievements of broader pro-democracy groups and experts and professionals in the mass media. Under the new Press Law, the newly-established Press Council is responsible for safeguarding press freedom from external intervention, for drafting and supervising the implementation of a journalistic code of ethics, and for seeking resolutions to public complaints on news reports. Members of the Council consist of independent individuals from relevant backgrounds—journalism, management, and academia. Pursuant to the Broadcasting Laws, the government established the Indonesian Broadcast Commission as an independent, state regulatory body on 26 December 2003. The Broadcasting Commission has more power than the Council, and for some media practitioners, its power is excessive and unconstitutional.[5]

The Broadcasting Law No. 32/2002 has suffered legal challenges from associations of media companies, some of which have gone as far as the Constitutional Court. Even after the Court handed down a verdict that satisfied all contending parties in July 2004, new disputes among the Commission, media companies and the government arose over the more procedural issues of a technical enforcement. As a social institution, the media still face a long battle. Regardless of the final outcome of this legal battle, it is fair to say that Indonesia has made giant steps towards liberalising the media. The battle itself is testimony to the scope and quality of Indonesia's newly-acquired liberal democracy.

It must be admitted, liberalisation has not been even, nor has it meant the same thing to all people. Reform in the print media has been more difficult. While the liberated television has been heavily criticised and censured, mainly for its sensationalism (through showing 'pornographic', 'uneducational', and 'violent' images), the print media have been a frequent target of legal threats and libel cases. Unlike the Broadcasting Law, the new Press Law governing the print media has enjoyed barely any recognition or effective power. Despite significant increased remuneration for journalists and greater freedom for their professional associations, journalists have not been much better protected at their places of work than than they were during the Suharto era. Management as well as individual journalists continue to be subject to assault, intimidation and violence from state and non-state agents.

On 20 February 2008, the Depok State Court found Bersihar Lubis, a senior journalist with the daily *Koran Tempo*, guilty for using an 'offensive' word—*dungu* (stupid)—in an opinion column dated 17 March 2007.[6] The word was used to describe the Attorney-General's decision to ban the government-sponsored history textbook for secondary schools, because it did not conform to the New Order's official history of its rise to power in which the Indonesian Communist Party is blamed for the so-called 'abortive coup attempt' in 1965. Such prosecutions occurred frequently during the New Order, victimising hundreds of citizens. Seen as a legally-flawed trial, the 2007 case provoked angry protests from many media outlets, journalist associations, the National Commission of Human Rights and individuals. Although these protests did not succeed in getting the case dropped or the defendant's acquittal, they seemed to have a significant impact upon the presiding judges in their decision making and sentence mitigation. The court sentenced the defendant to one month's imprisonment, but he didn't actually have to spend any time in jail; instead he was given a three-month probation period of good conduct.

A more alarming incident is the Supreme Court decision on 13 September 2007 in favour of Suharto in his legal battle against the magazine *Time* over its coverage (24 May 1999) of his allegedly ill-gotten wealth. Suharto had previously lost the case twice when it was investigated by the Central Jakarta District Court and then by the High Court upon the plaintiff's appeal. Overturning these decisions, the judges of the Supreme Court, chaired by a retired army general, demanded that the magazine and its seven journalists print an apology and pay Rp1,000,000,000 (US$106 million) to the plaintiff. *Time* has decided to continue the legal battle against the Indonesian ruling.

Before the above ruling, Indonesia witnessed another dispute between Tomy Winata and Indonesia's most prestigious news magazine, the Jakarta-based *Tempo*, and its sister daily *Koran Tempo*. In late January 2004, the South Jakarta court declared the daily *Koran Tempo* guilty of running a libellous report and discrediting a New Order tycoon, Tomy Winata, who was suspected of having interests in a wide range of industries, including illegal gambling. The court ruled that the accused had to pay compensation, the unprecedented amount of US$1 million, and to make a public apology in eight newspapers, six magazines and 12 television stations, including the international broadcasters, CNN and CNBC, for three consecutive days. It also ruled that failure to comply would entail a further Rp10 million (US$1,190) per day fine. This shocking verdict came within weeks after the same daily was found guilty in a separate libel case filed by another New Order tycoon, a textiles manufacturer, Marimutu Sinivasan. In this verdict, the judges demanded that the daily print an immediate full-page apology, the contents of which would be decided by the plaintiff, in 20 newspapers, 12 magazines, and nine television networks, or again, face a fine of Rp10 million (US$1,190) per day.

But it has not stopped there. The daily *Koran Tempo* belongs to the media-holding company, the Tempo Group, whose principal publication, *Tempo*, was sued by Tomy Winata and Marimutu Sinivasan in other libel cases. The total compensation that Mr Winata was seeking in six separate libel cases from the holding company amounted to Rp342 billion (US$40.7 million). In September 2004 Bambang Harymurti, *Tempo*'s Chief Editor was sentenced to one year imprisonment in a newly-added defamation case filed by Tomy Winata. He was released pending an appeal and was acquitted on 9 February 2006 by the Supreme Court.

This all suggests that Indonesia's democratisation is gradual, with intermittent setbacks, but, overall, I argue that it has been consistent in its progression. Unfortunately, in most of the cases above, only the setbacks were widely reported in the media, especially outside Indonesia. The familiar aphorism 'no news is good news' has also been attested to in the case of the controversial publication of the Indonesian version of *Playboy* and the anti-pornography bill. While reporters of the commercial media were compelled to cover the attack by some Islamist groups on the *Playboy* office building and the legal indictment of the editor for allegedly publishing indecent material, none of them was interested in reporting the court's decision to declare the editor not guilty, which has put an end to the controversy. The extremely popular television show Newsdotcom, also known as 'Republik Mimpi', became news in Australia only after its stinging parody of the current and former heads of state in Indonesia drew a legal threat of defamation from the Minister of Information.[7] At the same time, Abu Bakar Bashir who remains little-known in Indonesia, has become an icon of terrorism in the foreign media.

Democracy and liberalisation are not the same thing. Even if we focus our discussion on liberalisation, we can safely argue that freedom of expression in Indonesia deserves more recognition than is usually noted, let alone appreciated, both inside and outside Indonesia. The degree to which media liberalisation in Indonesia has generated better quality journalism is open to debate. Disagreements often originate from different sets of expectations or bases for comparison. Are we comparing the performance of Indonesia's media today with that of the media under the New Order? Or are we comparing it with its counterparts elsewhere in the region? Or are we comparing what they have actually produced with what we think they could and should have produced? These are difficult questions. A search for a satisfactory answer is beyond the scope of this chapter.

With rare exceptions, such as the work of Krishna Sen and David Hill (2000), most scholarly studies on Indonesia's media present an unbalanced portrayal, which emphasises the dark sides—bribery, censorship, and assaults against journalists—and which is based on a set of highly questionable presumptions and the sense of superiority of someone coming from a liberal democracy. The following two sets of issues illustrate my point.

First, frequent disputes and controversies in Indonesia, following the provocative attempts by the powerful to silence critics or to repress media, are too often confused with the reality. These repressive attempts are generally assumed to be effective and all-consuming, leading analysts to conclude that the Indonesia mediascape is dominated by repression. It does not usually occur to the analysts that these controversies may, in fact, demonstrate how the newly-liberated media crusaders have successfully pushed the limits of their new liberty to the farthest possible extent; an extent most likely uncommon or unseen in liberal democracies elsewhere, most notably during the enforcement of draconian laws in the so-called 'War Against Terrorism'. Alternatively, the controversy may simply be an index of the frantic desperation and the unpreparedness on the part of the intimidated elite and the conservative segments of the population in dealing with newly and aggressively liberalised media.

The fact that such controversies have taken place, often over an extended period, with great passion, and involving a huge number of citizens with diverse backgrounds demonstrates the dynamics of a robust democracy so lacking in many societies where liberal democracy is more often assumed and mythologised, and seldom tested. Interestingly, a lack of such controversy has been widely interpreted against a double standard. There is usually a quiet, but deeply running, assumption in English-language analyses that the absence or lack of controversy over issues of freedom of speech in liberal democracies is unequivocally a sign of well-protected freedom of speech, rather than a sign of a range of possible situations, including public disempowerment, apathy or the dullness of the media. But the same lack or absence of controversy is usually assumed to be evidence of severe repression of civil liberty, when it is identified in countries like China or Singapore.[8]

All the above requires a critical re-examination of the powerful and insidious assumptions underlying the many familiar analyses of contemporary Indonesia in the broader context of its history and democratisation. A set of problematic assumptions and prejudices, plus the general overlooking of the historical connectedness between the New Order period and what has followed, appears to be responsible for the widespread disappointment in post-authoritarian Indonesia among citizens and their observers alike. Another possible source of such low morale is intellectual in nature, namely problematic assumptions about inherent qualities of democracy, to which the next section will be devoted.

Democracy as fetish[9]

While sharing the general wisdom that democracy remains the best model of governance that we know today, I find it both surprising and worrisome to see how discussions of democracy—both among scholars and others—in the past few decades have commonly made far-reaching assumptions about the merits of democracy. This is especially true when such discussions take place among people who see themselves as members of a liberal and democratic community of some sort, analysing other societies. On the basis of an extensive review, Julia Paley (2002:469–96) suggests that one notable set of exceptions to that general observation can be found among recent works in anthropology and others with some anthropology-derived insights. It is hard to resist the suspicion that self-delusion or ethno-centricism may be at work among many democratic-minded people of the late 20th and early 21st centuries.[10]

Surely, the term 'democracy' means different things among a range of people. It is also used differently for different purposes. For instance, among many political activists across Asia, the term 'democracy' has often been used in their banners, slogans, or in naming their groups and their goals. Understandably in such situations, democracy is evoked without the need, intention, or invitation that it be examined in any critical or scholarly fashion. In these cases 'democracy' is taken for granted as a kind of magic wand to solve many kinds of problems; a tool that is assumed to be inherently unproblematic in itself.

But, even within that specific domain of activism, it remains to be explained why 'democracy', instead of other key terms, should have been chosen by a wide range of activist groups with different and contradictory interests in their banners, rallying cries and slogans, as well as in their choice of name. I suspect this has something to do with the already authoritative—perhaps hegemonic—status enjoyed by that term, as a result of its use by the more powerful and privileged institutions and members of social groups (including scholars, journalists, and politicians), regardless of whether or not they have intended it to achieve that status. Perhaps there is no conspiracy or concerted propaganda to bring 'democracy' to its current salience, but one cannot assume that the term's prominence is purely accidental. While these privileged groups often distinguish themselves from the activists, and although they claim and have enjoyed the respect of others for speaking 'truth' in a disinterested, measured and critical manner relative to activities in their street rallies, their use of 'democracy' is barely distinguishable or any more critical than the activists.

'Democracy' is but one of the most recent terms in the series of key terms in Indonesian studies. In the last few decades it has enjoyed the status comparable to that of 'development' in the preceding decades in the middle of the 20th century, and 'modernity' before that. For nearly 100 years, countries like Indonesia have been an object of scholarly analysis by Indonesians and foreign observers alike, primarily as a case of a people lacking something deemed to be unproblematic and universally desirable, which 'the West' can assist it in getting. Until about the 1960s, Indonesia was studied primarily as a country that needed, but lacked, 'modernity'. For roughly the next two decades, Indonesia was primarily described as a 'developing' country, implying its presumably regrettable lack and its predestined future, namely industrialisation and incorporation into world capitalism. Now it is a country that is seen primarily as having the potential to be the world's third largest democracy, if it follows in the footsteps of established 'modern', 'developed' and democratic nations on the other side of the globe.

Both in Indonesia and in Indonesian studies, there has for too long been too much adulation of democracy as a kind of promised land, or as a gate that leads to heavenly peace, prosperity and happiness. The democratising realities of Indonesia, as elsewhere around the globe, have betrayed and contradicted this powerful myth among scholars, journalists, activists and many others. (For a review of 'democracy deficit' across the Americas, European Union and beyond, see Paley (2002:470)). But old habits do not die easily. Of the few scholars to escape from the spell of this myth, the late Daniel Lev was one with special expertise on Indonesia. 'No-one', he warned us, 'should fall into the trap of supposing that it is the real thing, or even that the real thing is desirable' (2005:351). He contended that the term democracy should 'probably be banned or a charge levied on its use by serious students of politics' (2005:349). But as he explained, it is not easy for any one of us in a liberal democracy to give up the delusion of democracy because it make us 'feel better about ourselves' (2005:349), while pitying or despising others who live in what appears to us as undemocratic societies.[11]

According to Paley (2002:473), during the Cold War 'democracy functioned ideologically as the antithesis to Soviet communism and was deployed in US foreign policy...After the Cold War...democracy [was linked to] free market economics.' So hegemonic has the propaganda of democracy become that even those who have been frequently and unfairly attacked as dangerously undemocratic feel the need to develop a counter-argument within the framework of the attacking party. I cannot remember how many times I have discovered, with unease, serious and lengthy papers prepared in earnest by colleagues and students alike to the effect that Islam and democratic values are not or not necessarily incompatible. 'The Indonesian case is not often enough cited as proof, if proof were needed, that Muslim-majority countries can create democratic political systems' (Ward 2007:15). It is as if Islam is respectable and credible only if it is proven to be 'democratic', and only after the world recognises this.

As should be clear from the foregoing discussion, the problem with democracy is not that it comes from a foreign land and is incompatible with what the New Order state spokespersons propagated as Indonesia's authentic political tradition (Bourchier 1997:157–85). Rather, the problem with democracy lies in the fact that it has not been universally accepted either as a concept or as practice; it was not even accepted in Western Europe until about a century ago. To quote Arblaster (1994:7):

> For most of its long history, from the classical Greeks to the present day, democracy was seen by the enlightened and educated [in the West] as one of the worst types of government and society imaginable. Democracy was more or less synonymous with 'the rule of the mob'.

It should be no surprise that for a long time in many Asian countries, a significant portion of the people are prepared to compromise their freedom of expression and association for added prosperity in a political order that outsiders disparage as 'authoritarian' in character (for Southeast Asia, see Hadiz (2000:10–33) and Stubbs (2001:37–54); for Burma, see Alamgir (1997:333–50); for China and Taiwan, see Shi (2000:53–83)). One would suspect that this inclination is by no means peculiarly Asian; under similar circumstances others might well do likewise.

The success of propaganda for democracy and the fantasies it inspires has most likely been a source of disillusionment and distress among analysts when looking at today's Indonesia. Unless that myth is adequately deconstructed among Indonesians, we continue to live and work in the delusion of 'democracy jihad'.[12] In the years to come, as industrialisation expands and consolidates, the Indonesian media, like its parliamentary politics, will likely become more dull, commercially driven, and lacking in controversy. Until then, I would still see Indonesia as being in a state of bearable lightness of democracy.

Notes

1   The author is grateful to Andy Fuller for his editorial suggestions and comments on an earlier version of the essay. The title of this chapter is indebted to Milan Kundera's *The unbearable lightness of being* (1984).

   Indonesia is clearly democratic within the 'minimalist' definition of democracy and more democratic than many in Asia-Pacific region. The phrase 'minimalist definition of democracy' refers to some of the most basic and formal elements of democracy that constitute the necessary conditions. These elements include open, regular, regulated and independently-administered elections to choose and change governments, through a relatively fair, transparent and free contest for votes among competing political parties within the bounds of previously-agreed rules and procedures. These necessary conditions are deemed insufficient by others, especially advocates of the so-called maximalist definitions of 'democracy', who also disagree among themselves with regard to what additional elements should be included in a definition of 'democracy' to make it more acceptable. However, as will be elaborated in the next section, contemporary democracy in Indonesia has more qualities than the minimalist definition requires. Suffice it to note here that, in contrast to liberal democracy in countries such as Australia, Indonesia's elections are not compulsory and yet they have always attracted no less than 90% of eligible voters to cast ballots. The fact that certain anti-democratic elements continue to exist in post-authoritarian Indonesia (just as in most liberal democracies whose democratic status is often taken for granted) does not invalidate its status as a fully democratic nation.

2   Not even a modest survey of recent literature is intended here. For a random selection of the recent reviews, misgivings, and assessments which emphasise the imperfection of Indonesian democracy, see Andrew, Roesad and Edwin (2005:53–77), Freedman (2007:195–216), Kim, Liddle and Said (2006:247–68), Slatter (2006:208–13) and Webber (2006:396–42).

3   According to one survey in late 2003 conducted by the Indonesian Survey Institute some 60.3% of 2,160 respondents (from 372 villages and cities in 32 provinces) preferred Suharto's New Order political system to the current one. Only 25.2% of respondents had the opposite view. A separate survey a month earlier by Charney Research of New York and AC Nielsen Indonesia and commissioned by The Asia Foundation resulted in a similar outcome; 53% of eligible voters in the 2004 elections 'preferred a strong leader like former president Suharto, even if this meant that rights and freedoms would be reduced' (Kurniawan 2003; Gazali 2003).

4   Facts and figures in this and the next four paragraphs have been presented in an earlier version (Heryanto and Hadiz 2005:251–75).

5   The Commission not only has the power to set the code of ethics for practitioners in radio and television broadcasting, but also has purview over a wide range of regulatory matters, including media ownership, licensing, and penalties for irregular practices. In reaction to these new constraints that threatened their will to retain power and reap huge profit, some within the media industry have alleged that the Commission has shown an inclination to be as repressive as the New Order's Department of Information.

6   The court found the defendant guilty under Article 207 of the Penal Code (offensive statements to state officials). In the past, the New Order government penalised hundreds of journalists, artists and student activists for violating a series of 'hate-sowing' articles inherited from Dutch colonial law dating from the early 20th century. These articles survived a series of amendments during the first few years of post-New Order period. Some, but not all, of these articles were eliminated by the Constitutional Court on 5 December 2006, the day before the same Court annulled the formation of the National Commission of Truth and Reconciliation.

7   See the special report by SBS TV on 6 June 2007. It is significant how host George Negus introduced the report on the Indonesian controversy with the following words: 'In Australia, political satire has had an incredibly rich history. Then again, we have been a democracy for over 100 years. But apparently, to our north, our giant neighbour Indonesia—not even a decade since the fall of the Suharto dictatorship—finds itself glued to a television show that actually lampoons the nation's politicians.' For an analysis of the program, see Jurriëns (2008).

8   I recall a minor disagreement I had with a colleague in Brisbane in 2004 about the significance of the banning of the three Jakarta weeklies (*Tempo*, *Editor* and *Detik*). Like many observers before him, he saw the incident with alarm, believing that it showed the New Order regime had both the power and interest to take back the promise of political openness once offered to the people. In contrast, I saw the incident as a new light of hope signifying the regime's panic in the face of a crisis of elite cohesion and legitimacy and its desperate attempt to restore the appearance of being in control.

9   The phrase 'democracy as fetish' was used by Begoña Aretxaga (2000:48) in a different context and with different meanings in her analysis of Spain, and commented on by Paley (2002:477).

10 The other side of the coin is corruption. This is another important key term in the study of contemporary Indonesia. Not unlike democracy, corruption is used liberally far and wide by many analysts to explain what is wrong with Indonesia, barely (if at all) with a moment of self-doubt or critical examination of whether something is wrong or corrupted in the concept of corruption itself as an analytical tool. Anthropologist Nils Bubant is aware of the risk of such uncritical analyses of cases in Indonesia (2006: 427). However, despite his own awareness, Bubant attributes increased corruption specifically to 'new democracies'.

11 'The less we know about a country or region or group', Lev (2005:346) noted, 'the more likely it is that [terms such as democracy]...will shape what we think we know.'

12 The term 'democracy jihad' first came to my attention in the writing of Aung-Thwin (2001:483–505). Although I find Aung-Thwin's phrase useful, I do not necessarily agree with many points in his analysis of Burma.

chapter six

The incredible shrinking Pancasila: nationalist propaganda and the missing ideological legacy of Suharto

Robert Cribb

The old man died. They buried him.

On the morning of Monday 28 January 2008, a military plane took off from Jakarta's Halim Air Force Base with the body of Suharto, President of Indonesia for 32 years, former commander of the Indonesian Army's Strategic Reserve, former commander of the Central Java Diponegoro Division, former revolutionary military officer, former sergeant in the Dutch colonial army, former village boy.

The plane landed in Solo and a military convoy took the body on a narrow asphalt road leading eastwards and uphill, past the village of Matesih, to a place called Astana Giribangun, (Palace of the Risen Mountain). There, at 12.25 pm, the remains of the former president were consigned to the Suharto family mausoleum, a low building with wide eaves and a high central spire in traditional Javanese style.

The building had waited a long time to receive its distinguished occupant. Construction began in 1974, the year that President Suharto had faced his first serious political challenge in the form of the Malari riots. Ostensibly directed against the visiting Japanese Prime Minister Tanaka Kakuei, the riots were widely seen as an outpouring of discontent with Suharto's economic policies. Following the displacement of President Sukarno in 1966–67, Suharto had implemented policies of accelerated economic development that involved fiscal stabilisation and massive investment in infrastructure, funded by foreign aid and by revenues from the sale of oil and timber. Suharto's policies pulled Indonesia out of the economic misery of the final years of Sukarno's rule, but they left victims—families evicted from squatter settlements for construction projects, workers given no opportunity to pursue higher wages in the absence of free trade unions. And they had beneficiaries. Those who agreed to work with the New Order, especially in its upper echelons, found opportunity, sometimes abundant opportunity, to acquire wealth through corruption. It would be another three years before the pop group Bimbo satirised the new rich of the New Order in the song 'Tante Sun', but in 1974 the signs were there of a new gap between rich and poor, even if the poor were much less poor than they had been (Mortimer 1974).

In 1974, the year he began to build Astana Giribangun, Suharto saw off his last credible challenger from within the Indonesian military elite. The now-forgotten General Sumitro, a corpulent, moustachioed caricature of a Third World general, had begun to map out a populist alliance with student groups, seemingly as a prelude to telling Suharto at some point that his time was up. Sumitro was head of KOPKAMTIB, the New Order's military command for security and order, and he seemed ready to replicate the pattern of Third World military politics in which each former military president is displaced by his successor in the army. But Suharto had outmanoeuvred him and he spent his days after 1974 playing golf and writing political commentary (Jenkins 1984).

Also in 1974, Suharto abandoned the dour no-politics conceit of the early New Order and gave Indonesia a state ideology. As the basis for this ideology he chose the Pancasila, five broad principles that had been incorporated into the preamble of the first constitution of newly-independent Indonesia in 1945. Formulated by Indonesia's first president, Sukarno, the Pancasila was a declaration of programmatic nationalism. One of the five principles—the unity of Indonesia—spoke directly to land and soil, those traditional exemplars of national identity, but the others—belief in God, humanity, democracy, and social justice—had no specific link to the people of the archipelago. They contained no hint of ethnicity, or even history. Rather, they were noble universal principles that Sukarno presented as the basis for a national identity transcending simple hostility to colonialism.

But incorporating the Pancasila into the Constitution's preamble was not just an assertion of nobility; it was also an act of exclusion. Inserting belief in God—whether the God of Christians or the God of Muslims—into the Constitution meant that Indonesia could not be an Islamic state, despite the fact that around 90% of its population were Muslims. Blocking that road, in turn, meant that the Indonesian state would be alien to those of its Muslim subjects who believed that Muslims could only dwell in the place of peace, a *Darussalam*, if they lived under Islamic law. An Islamic state in Indonesia would have alienated still more Indonesians, not just believers in other religions but also Muslims whose Islam did not require Islamic law; nonetheless the Pancasila took its second incarnation as a device to exclude fundamental Islam from the idiom of national politics. During the 1950s, the Pancasila took on a third identity, this time against communism. As the Indonesian Communist Party (PKI) grew in popularity, belief in God became a bulwark against the supposed atheism of the communists. They could not, it was asserted, be true Indonesians without believing in God.

In 1965–66, Suharto crushed the PKI and pasted the Pancasila label in front of democracy to characterise his undemocratic order, but mass killing and mass detention turned out to be a far more effective way of excluding communism from the national idiom. A heavily-orchestrated electoral and parliamentary system excluded fundamentalist Islam nearly as effectively, and the Pancasila was hardly more than a distant flag for the early years of Suharto's rule (Nishimura 1995). Even government officials, asked to list the five principles, would struggle to recall more than three or four. In 1974, however, the Pancasila entered its fourth incarnation as a corporatist ideology for the Suharto regime.

The mausoleum that Suharto constructed in 1974 was an architectural hybrid. The form of the mausoleum resembled the palace (*kraton*) of the minor Mangkunegaran royal family with which Suharto's wife was loosely connected, but the high peak of its roof recalled some of the traditional architecture of eastern Indonesia (Pemberton 2000). The Pancasila of 1974, the year of the mausoleum, of the Malari riots, and of the fall of Sumitro, was also a hybrid. Sukarno's universalist formulation was recast as essentialist Indonesian culture, dug out of the Indonesian earth with no input or inspiration from outside (Antlöv 2005:46–47). A committee chaired by former vice-president and nationalist leader Mohammad Hatta began to shape what became known as P4, the *Pedoman Penghayatan dan Pengamalan Pancasila* (Guide for the Realisation and Implementation of Pancasila), which was formally adopted by parliament in 1978. Rather than working as a device to exclude specific sections of Indonesian society from full acceptance as Indonesians, this new Pancasila was devised as a guide to behaviour. The P4 identified 36 behavioural norms (*butir*, literally 'nuggets') said to be derived from the Pancasila:

Belief in God (four nuggets)

- Belief in and devotion to God, according to each person's respective religion and beliefs on the basis of a just and civilised humanity
- Respect and co-operation between believers and followers of different religions and beliefs for the sake of social harmony
- Mutual respect for the freedom to worship according to respective religions and beliefs
- Not forcing one religion or belief on others

Humanity (eight nuggets)

- Recognise the equal status, equal rights and equal duties of all human beings
- Love each other as human beings
- Develop respectful attitudes
- Don't behave cruelly to others
- Give the highest respect to human values
- Be fond of undertaking humanitarian acts
- Have the courage to defend truth and justice
- The Indonesian people are a part of humankind as a whole and therefore should develop attitudes of respect and co-operation towards other peoples

Unity of Indonesia (five nuggets)

- Place the unity, one-ness, interests and welfare of the people and the state above personal or group interests
- Be willing to sacrifice oneself for the interests of the people and the state
- Love one's country and people
- Be proud of being Indonesian and be one with the country
- Promote social interaction for the sake of the unity and one-ness of the people, based on the principle *Bhinneka Tunggal Ika* (Unity in diversity)

Democracy (seven nuggets)

- Give priority to the interests of state and society
- Don't force your will on other people
- Give priority to consultation and discussion (*musyawarah*) when taking decisions in the common interest.
- Consultation and discussion so as to achieve consensus based on family spirit
- With good faith and a sense of responsibility accept and implement the decisions of the community
- Consultation and discussion are carried out with sound reasoning and according to a glorious inner heart
- Decisions must be morally consistent with the will of God, and must exalt the status of human beings and the values of truth and justice

Social justice (12 nuggets)

- Develop glorious actions that reflect the attitude and atmosphere of family and mutual self-help
- Have a just attitude
- Ensure a balance between rights and duties
- Respect the rights of others
- Help other people
- Reject the use of force against others
- Don't be wasteful
- Don't live extravagantly
- Don't do things that harm the public interest
- Work hard
- Appreciate the work of others
- Strive together to achieve progress that is equitable and socially just.[1]

In 1978, courses to instruct government officials in these fine points of the Pancasila were introduced, followed not long after by an extensive program of Pancasila Moral Education (Pendidikan Moral Pancasila, PMP) in all educational institutions. In 1985, Suharto had the Pancasila declared the *azas tunggal* (sole basic principle) for all social organisations, other than businesses, in Indonesia. This law required even religious organisations to place the Pancasila ahead of their basic beliefs, at least in a formal sense, and it aroused great antagonism, especially from Muslim circles (Bourchier & Hadiz 2003:14, 82–96).

The ideological heart of Suharto's Pancasila was a conception of Indonesia as an organic society. The consequence of this organicism was that there were no natural conflicts in Indonesian society; conflicts arose out of the intrusion of alien values (communism, liberalism and the like) and out of egoism, the selfish placing of individual interests ahead of those of society. In making this contrast between the constructive collective interest of society and the destructiveness of competitive individualism, the Pancasila placed itself both in the tradition of President Sukarno's condemnation of 'free-fight' liberalism and in the vanguard of the so-called 'Asian values debate' (Barr 2004). PMP emphasised, therefore, subordinating individual interest to the common good, and avoiding conflict and maintaining social harmony as absolute social goods (Parker 1992:95–116; Kammen 1995:147–54).

Indonesia's sixth president, retired General Susilo Bambang Yudhoyono, delivered a brief speech at Suharto's funeral on 28 January 2008:

Honoured guests and the whole of the Indonesian people, wherever they may be, *inna lillahi wa inna ilaihi roji`un* [Io, we belong to Allah, and to Allah we return], with the deepest sorrow, we the whole Indonesian people are gathered here today to mark the passing of Retired General HM Suharto, second President of the Republic of Indonesia.

The deceased [*almarhum*] returned peacefully to the mercy of Allah on Sunday 27 January 2008 at 13.10, Western Indonesian Time, in the Central Pertamina Hospital, Jakarta.

We have lost one of our best sons, a faithful fighter, a true soldier and an honoured statesman.

We have come here to the family tomb of Astana Giribangun at Karanganyar to pay our final respects at this state ceremony.

We carry out this ceremony as a sign of honour and appreciation from the state and the government for the selfless service and conscientious achievements of the deceased to the state and the people during his life.

As we all know, the deceased, born in Yogyakarta on 8 June 1921, devoted his whole life to the people and the state.

He had a long career in the military, politics and government.

History records that during the National Revolution of 1945–1949 the deceased struggled unyieldingly to expel the colonialists to realise and defend the sovereignty of the people and of the young state.

History also notes a most monumental act of struggle: when the deceased and other fighters launched the General Attack of 1 March 1949 and occupied the city of Yogyakarta.

This important event was a weighty and powerful contribution to the negotiations that ended in recognition of the sovereignty of the Republic of Indonesia.

Following the National Revolution, in 1962, when this country was struggling to liberate West Irian, the deceased returned to fulfil the call of his state by carrying out glorious duty as head of the Mandala Command.

History has already recognised this event as a successful fusion between diplomacy and armed force.

In 1965, when our nation was tested once again by the G30S PKI affair, once again took up his duty to save the integrity of the state, the integrity of the nation and to restore security and order.

During his time in government, that is, after being appointed President of the Republic of Indonesia on 27 March 1968, the deceased unyieldingly led the national development program that rested on the Developmental Trilogy [*Trilogi Pembangunan*], that is, Stability, Growth and Equality.

The many outcomes and successes that were achieved by the government which the deceased led brought about the fact that the Indonesian people, step, by step, became increasingly advanced [*maju*] and increasingly prosperous.

Honoured guests:

It is appropriate that, with honesty and with pure hearts, we acknowledge the deceased's many services to the people and to the state.

Nonetheless, we are conscious that as an ordinary human being and as a leader he could not be without mistakes and shortcomings.

None of us slaves of Allah is perfect in this world.

So let us, as a great-hearted people express our sincere thanks and offer our respect and great appreciation for the achievements and services which the deceased has rendered to people and state.

On this important occasion, I would also like to invite all Indonesians to pray for the deceased so that he will cross safely to the side of Allah the All Powerful, reflecting his struggle, his sacrifice and spiritual devotion.

We pray that Allah will grant fortitude and patience to the family of the deceased and that they will accept his departure with sincerity and acquiescence.

Finally, praying to Allah, let us release the deceased so that he can meet the Creator with serenity.

And let us pray to Allah that He will accept the deceased's devotion and forgive his sins.

Travel safely [*selamat jalan*], Father of Development [*Bapak Pembangunan*]. We pray that you are peacefully at the side of Allah.

Thank you.[2]

It was a speech remarkable for its faint praise of the man who had ruled Indonesia for 32 years. The President was careful to share recognition for Suharto's achievements with other fighters, with diplomats, with the government that he had led. His account of the economic progress under the New Order—Suharto's supreme claim to greatness—is restrained at best. Suharto's devotion to his state and people is emphasised almost as much as the results of that devotion. The speech reads as an act of formal duty, not a heartfelt tribute to the President's former commander-in-chief. The reference to Suharto's shortcomings and mistakes, too, may have been a routine expression of religious submissiveness, but Susilo Bambang Yudhoyono offered no hint of justification for the mistakes and everyone listening to the speech would have thought of the corruption case against the former president that was still unresolved at the time of his death. Perhaps they also thought of the half million communists, the tens of thousands of Timorese and Papuans, the thousands of Acehnese and the other dissidents who had perished under Suharto's auspices.

The most remarkable feature of the funeral, however, was the absence of the Pancasila. The ideology that had marked the New Order for 20 years was neither mentioned nor alluded to in the presidential speech. Nor were the narrow roads to Astana Giribangun lined with Suhartoists asserting that their leader's ideology would live on as inspiration after his death. The very term 'Suhartoism' remains an alien one in Indonesian politics.[3] The Pancasila lives on, but it has returned to its second incarnation as code for the rejection of an Islamic state in Indonesia. In the 1999 and 2004 elections, parties which did not choose Islam (or codes for Islam) as their formal basis tended to choose the Pancasila as a sign of what they were not (Pompe 1999).

Over the course of 20 years, Indonesians spent millions of hours studying the Pancasila. Students were not permitted to progress to the next grade, officials were not promoted unless they passed the compulsory training in the state ideology. Millions of pages were printed and tens of thousands of broadcast hours were used to disseminate the Pancasila message to every corner of the archipelago. And yet the Pancasila has disappeared as an ideological force.

The disappearance is all the more remarkable given the resilience of other aspects of New Order indoctrination, especially hostility to communism. The vehemence of hostility to communism in contemporary Indonesia is remarkable, given the global retreat of communism as an intellectual and political force and the shameful circumstances of the murder of half a million members of the PKI in 1965–6 (Heryanto 1999:147–177). In 2000, there was widespread public outrage when President Abdurrahman Wahid proposed abolishing Resolution No. 25/1966 which had been passed by Provisional People's Consultative Assembly (MPRS) on 5 July 1966, outlawing the PKI and banning the teaching of Marxist-Leninist ideology.[4] Although it is not difficult to find reasons why the New Order wished to sustain the anti-communist paranoia of its early years, the puzzle is why it was not able to sustain the Pancasila to the same effect.

The explanation lies in the special character of Pancasila propaganda. We think of propaganda as having the purpose of persuading people into a view that they would not otherwise have had—a generally political purpose. We know that Suharto made deft use of anti-communist propaganda in the weeks after the so-called 30th September Movement coup in Jakarta on 1 October 1965. Though we cannot now examine the actual workings of this propaganda, it seems that the carefully manufactured stories of the torture and sexual mutilation of anti-communist generals, together with manufactured rumours that communists in general were planning to slaughter their neighbours contributed significantly to the willingness of ordinary Indonesians to take part in the mass killings that followed (Drakeley 2000). The propaganda of 1965 was plausible in an atmosphere of profound political uncertainty and antagonism.

What, then, is one to make of the Pancasila propaganda that enjoined Indonesians to reject the use of force against others, to avoid waste and not to live extravagantly? Around them they could see these injunctions flouted daily by the very people who were communicating them. Even though Indonesian elites have traditionally despised the masses for their 'stupidity' (*kebodohan*), the Pancasila propaganda format seems egregiously unconvincing.

It is likely, however, that it was never meant to convince, or at least never meant to convince comprehensively in the way that, for instance, communists in China demanded thoroughgoing belief in party doctrine. Rather, apart from the odd useful effect it might have on the unusually receptive, the Pancasila functioned as 'white noise'. It was quasi-ideological chatter intended to fill the space in Indonesian public life that might otherwise be occupied by serious, ideologically informed discussion.

Throughout its history, Pancasila has confused observers of Indonesia. How could such a bland set of principles take so central a place in national political discourse? The answer is that it was never truly an ideology. Even in its most elaborated form under the New Order, it was a device to mark who would be included in and excluded from the Indonesian project. Its decline after 1998 partly reflected the discrediting of the New Order, but its disappearance has much more to do with a transformation in the politics of exclusion that has taken place over the last ten years.

There are two elements in this transformation. First is the introduction of democracy which has the great benefit of giving value to every voter. Authoritarian systems based on patronage, as the New Order was, rely on informal devices to ensure that people know their place, that they know who is in and who is out. The New Order's Pancasila was designed to impart this understanding to Indonesian society in general. Democracy has led by contrast to a more inclusive national discourse. One of the most encouraging developments in this respect has been the removal of formal discrimination against Indonesians of Chinese descent and the fact that the removal of this discrimination has provoked no hostile reaction, either from the elite or from the masses. Second, the introduction of far-reaching regional autonomy has created new contours of exclusion within Indonesia. As more and more important decisions are taken at a local level, the overwhelming importance of creating exclusionary devices at the centre has simply eroded. The importance of being *putra daerah* (a child of the local region) has intruded dramatically into local politics, and the inclusiveness of the national sphere can be valued as an alternative. These two elements in the transformation of Indonesian politics are enormously important in establishing generally-accepted conventions for accepting democratic procedures. Even if we can still sense the excitement and nobility of Sukarno's original idea of Pancasila, expressed in 1945 on the eve of Indonesian independence, we can recognise that the departure of the Pancasila is a good thing for Indonesian politics.

Implications for the future

Whenever a powerful, long-lasting ruler dies, we feel an urgent need for some kind of summary judgement. So it was when Suharto died in January 2008. When the destiny of a country has appeared to have been so tightly woven into the life of an individual man, we want to know what difference he really made and what his legacy to the future will be.

For the most part, the verdicts on Suharto sought to establish the balance between his achievements and his shortcomings. His achievements? Above all, Indonesia's spectacular economic growth since 1966, its transformation from one of the poorest countries of the world to a land where the vast majority of people experience a low to middling standard of living. Despite the crisis in the Indonesian economy in 1997 and after, the country is still in a far stronger economic position than at any time before Suharto came to power.

Alongside economic growth, public order. Only a shrinking minority of Indonesians recall the political atmosphere of late Guided Democracy, when shrill political confrontations dominated the news and violent clashes racked the countryside, when the Islamic revolution of the Darul Islam, far more destructive in terms of life and property than any of today's Islamist terror, had only just been brutally suppressed in rural West Java and South Sulawesi.

Alongside public order, a foreign policy in Southeast Asia which spearheaded the creation of ASEAN and Southeast Asia's remarkable long peace since the mid 1970s. The triviality and civility of the recent border dispute, for instance, with Malaysia over Sipadan and Ligitan is a striking contrast with the martial confrontations and the failed attempts at co-operation that dominated Southeast Asia before the creation of ASEAN.

Despite a faltering immediately after Suharto's fall from power in 1998, each of these achievements has proven to be durable. The succession crisis led some commentators to suggest that all the achievements of the Suharto era had suddenly crumbled to dust, but the reality is that Indonesia, even at the depths of the Asian financial crisis, was a far better run, more prosperous and civilised place than it had been when Suharto came to power. If we look only at Suharto's achievements we can see why his successor, Habibie, once enthusiastically described him as 'SGS' (Super Genius Suharto) (Emmerson 1999:315).

Yet against these achievements we can set massive shortcomings. Corruption, for one thing. By most measures Indonesia under Suharto was one of the most corrupt countries in the world, and the corruption went all the way to the top, in the form of the wealth that was creamed off to *yayasan* (supposedly charitable foundations) under Suharto's control. Suharto's personal lack of ostentation took an edge off this corruption—unlike other dictators he did not accumulate fast luxury cars or palaces—but he was the means by which funds that might otherwise have gone to the state for the benefit of the Indonesian people were devoted instead to his personal interests. And, of course, there were the Suharto children, predatory and hypocritical. Although he had a knack of choosing capable subordinates, he also tended to surround himself with an unsavoury collection of carpetbaggers, sycophants and opportunists who slurped up Indonesia's wealth for their own benefit.

Brutality for another thing. The killing of half a million Leftists in 1965–6, the intense violence against separatists and alleged separatists in East Timor, to which Indonesia had no reasonable title in international law, Aceh and Papua and the substantial violence at critical moments—in the *petrus* killings of the early 1980s and in Tanjung Priok in 1984. There have been many exaggerated claims of the number of victims in each of these conflicts and affairs, but even a conservative estimate gives us a figure of hundreds of thousands of people killed under the auspices of the New Order. Although it involved far fewer deaths, we have to consider also the New Order's vast protection racket run at the expense of Chinese Indonesians—the systematic extortion of protection money under threat of violence by Indonesian masses who were supposed to be viscerally anti-Chinese. Still more extensive than brutality was Suharto's crippling of public life in Indonesia, the suppression of free discussion by means of censorship and intimidation, the compromising of the parliamentary and election systems with a vast array of regulations that hypocritically preserved the form of democracy while draining that form of all meaning. When we look at the underside of the Suharto era like this, then we see sense in the summary judgement of *The Economist* (31 Jan. 2008), which called Suharto 'a crook and a tyrant'.

The contradiction between these two judgements was aptly reflected in the fact that Suharto's state funeral—the official recognition of his contributions to the nation—took place while the corruption case against him, a case which would have marked him definitively as a thief, was still pending. So how do we come to a verdict?

The most common approach is a kind of crude cost-benefit calculation. Suharto achieved economic growth and political stability at the cost of loss of life and political corruption. Depending on how we value the material welfare of the current generation and how we value the lives of previous generations, we come to a conclusion—a high price but worth paying, or too high a price. It is a calculation that tends to devalue past brutality in relation to current prosperity. Effectively we ask the living, how much of your prosperity would you surrender, if you could, to give life back to the dead, especially to dead communists?

I want to suggest that actually we don't need to do this at all. Physicists need to treat matter as both waves and particles. The two conceptions are not reconcilable, but we need each of them to work with matter in a theoretical way. Similarly, it should be possible to acknowledge both Suharto's achievements and his deep flaws without taking that final step of totting up a balance sheet. He was both a national hero and a devil.

The disappearance of a man like Suharto from the political order leaves huge uncertainty. Because his reach into the political system was so far-reaching, his absence created instability. But I think that we can actually feel enormously encouraged by the events that surrounded his death—no riots, no disturbances, almost no dogmatic reassertions of the values of the New Order. The money that he stole, the lives that he took, the lies that he told—all these things still matter, of course, but the big thing is that Suharto no longer hovers like a ghost over Indonesian politics. Indonesian society can move on and let the past become another country. And that is something to be deeply thankful for.

Notes

1   Author's translation of 'Ketetapan Majelis Permusyawaratan Rakyat Republik Indonesia Nomor II/MPR/1978 tentang Pedoman Penghayatan dan Pengamalan Pancasila (Ekaprasetia Pancakarsa)', www.mpr.go.id/pdf/ketetapan/ketetapan mpr thn 78.pdf. The 36 nuggets were later expanded to 45.

2   Author's translation of 'Sambutan Pemakaman Almarhum Jenderal Besar TNI (Purn) Haji Muhammad Soeharto, Karanganyar, Jawa Tengah, Senin, 28 Januari 2008', www.presidensby.info/index.php/pidato/2008/01/28/853.html .

3   On 1 March 2008, the Indonesian language term 'Suhartoisme' scored a mere 406 hits on Google while its English equivalent, 'Suhartoism', scored 207.

4   On the issue of rehabilitating the former communists, see Birks (2006).

chapter seven

Winning hearts and minds?
Religion and politics in post-Suharto Indonesia

Thomas Reuter

In this chapter I discuss how Indonesians have responded to the American War on Terror and to a succession of terrorist attacks by Islamic extremists, from the 11 September 2001 World Trade Center attacks to the 12 October 2002 Bali nightclub bombing and beyond, and how this response has shaped the politics of religion and the general political climate in Indonesia during the *reformasi* period.

The data for this chapter are derived mainly from my own ethnographic research on religious movements in Java from 1998 until the present.[1] In the course of this research I have been to many places in Java, where I have conversed with a wide range of people, from peasants to members of parliament, about issues relating to people's aspirations for the future of their nation. I was in Java to observe first-hand how different groups in Java reacted to 11 September 2001, the US-led attacks on Afghanistan and Iraq, and to further terrorist attacks abroad and at home.

My aim is to examine the extent to which the War on Terror and terrorist actions have influenced popular ideas about the usefulness of Islam as an alternative political model in the face of what many perceive as a loss of credibility for Indonesian nationalism, firstly because nationalism had been abused to legitimise authoritarianism under former president Suharto, and secondly, because the new nationalist leaders of the *reformasi* period appeared to be unable to establish political and economic stability. My thesis is that the combined effect of terrorism and the War on Terror has been a see-sawing of public opinion. The direction of these public opinion swings shows that most Indonesians in the newly democratic *reformasi* period have tended to oppose consistently those they perceive to be the party responsible for the dominant pattern of political violence and injustice at the time, whether the source of this violence be terrorism, the state, or the so-called 'world order' (Reuter 2003).

The other major trend I have observed, which is also reflected at the polls, is an increasing reflexivity and a slowly evolving immunity to manipulative hate propaganda with a religious flavour.

While Suharto had managed to keep a lid on Islamic politics through oppression until the early 1990s, and less so through engagement from then on, the new nationalist governments of the *reformasi* period appeared to be losing control even of their own Islamic spokespeople in the wake of 11 September 2001, and their security forces did not respond firmly to acts of terrorism within Indonesia. This lukewarm government response continued even after the 12 October 2002 terrorist attack in Bali. I believe the reason for this half-heartedness is that Indonesian politicians during *reformasi* rarely dared to buck the shifting trends of public opinion, particularly among the country's Muslim majority. Indonesian public opinion, in turn, has been strongly Islamised by international factors. One factor has been the dominant Western foreign policy toward the Islamic world in general, and towards Indonesia in particular, at that time. This policy was refracted, sometimes in a somewhat distorted manner, within Indonesian interpretations of world events. I would argue that Indonesian politics since 2001 has been prominently shaped by major world events, most notably by 11 September and the subsequent War on Terror. A second, but related, international factor is the gradual rise of a global Islamic movement, chiefly in Muslim countries with dictatorial secular governments and/or a recent history of foreign political intervention. Indonesia is one such country, but it is not alone. These two international factors have been mutually reinforcing and I will try to untangle this process in the following analysis.

International factors in Indonesia's politics of religion

On 11 September 2001, I was up late, packing my suitcase to catch an early flight destined for Java, an island with an overwhelming Muslim majority. As I witnessed the devastating attacks on the Pentagon and World Trade Center unfold live on American cable televison that night and heard the early reports that Islamic terrorists were held responsible, it became obvious to me that a US military strike would follow and that the whole fiasco would attract great interest from opportunists and demagogues on all sides of Indonesian politics. I also knew that these events would affect my own ethnographic research on minority groups of Javanese Hindus and nominal Muslims. Studies on religious minorities draw attention to issues of religious freedom and tolerance no matter where they are conducted, and nowhere more than in Indonesia, a country that has been swept by a wave of terrorist actions with a religious flavour and regional conflicts ever since the collapse of Suharto's military dictatorship in 1998. In the year 2000 alone, 250 bomb or fire attacks on houses of worship were reported in the media, not to mention the murders of individuals motivated by religious sentiment and the acts of verbal intimidation directed at religious minority groups, mostly Christians but also Hindus (see *Annual Report* 2001).

It is debatable whether the secular-minded New Order regime was simply successful in discouraging religious extremism for some time by shifting the public's focus on economic development, or whether Suharto's brutal and systematic persecution of political opponents was the cause of a politicisation of Islam. The latter is perhaps closer to the truth, at least with regard to the current wave of Islamic politics. As had been the case under Dutch colonial rule, religion provided the political opposition in Indonesia with some of the best cover for organising resistance under Suharto without attracting too much negative attention, until the time came to shift into gear and take political action. Recognising this danger in the 1990s, Suharto started to provide selected Islamic groups with financial and political support (Hefner 2000), aiming to appropriate, or at least appease, the Islamic movement. But, in the end, his politics of appeasement only helped to strengthen Islamic organisations. This, then, is a possible explanation of why religious affiliation, along with ethnic and other forms of particularism, became so integral to the rhetoric of political conflict in post-Suharto Indonesia (Bubandt 2002). There was simply no secular platform for political organisation available that would have been ready to fill the power vacuum left by Suharto. Apart from religious organisations, the only possible contender for power was Megawati's nationalist party, PDI (now PDI-P), which Suharto had allowed to exist as a toothless opposition party to help maintain an appearance of democracy. PDI suffered renewed persecution in the 1990s for trying to become a real opposition, and had earned some popular sympathy as a result.

Indonesia's difficulties with religiously-inspired terrorism, however, cannot be explained solely in domestic political terms. It also reflect the country's positioning in a broader, international scenario. Critics have argued for decades that Islamic terrorism, internationally, is the product of a longstanding United States foreign policy of intervention in Islamic countries, many of which are major oil producers. We know that the organisation blamed for that fateful attack on 11 September was a child of these policies too—Al-Qaeda had been created with American co-operation and support to serve as an armed Islamic resistance movement in Russian-occupied Afghanistan in the early 1980s and had co-operated militarily with the United States as recently as the Kosovo War (Ali 2002). All of this is more widely known and better reported in Indonesia than it is in mainstream Western mass media. Consequently, many Indonesians see in the political history of the 20th century a pattern of intervention and a global conspiracy directed at Indonesia and other Muslim nations.

Many of my Javanese informants believe that the United States Central Intelligence Agency helped to stage the communist coup attempt of 1965 that provided their protégé, General Suharto, with the excuse to remove Sukarno from power (Fuadi *et al* 2001; Yusi & Setiyardi 2001). Suharto and the military, many Javanese believe, were supported by the United States to prevent Indonesia from falling into line with international communism, which was spreading through Southeast Asia in the 1960s. That time it was 'mission accomplished', at the expense of up to a million Indonesian lives. When Sukarno's daughter became President 46 years later, there was much speculation that the United States had its eye on Indonesia once again. Some radical anti-Islamic nationalist groups imagined themselves as the beneficiaries of foreign help in their fantasies of waging a domestic 'War on [Islamic] Terror' in order to recreate a Javanese society based on a revived indigenous Javanese religion, and to have their revenge for 1965. Others on the left of politics rejected the idea of inviting further foreign intervention of this kind because they felt it would lead to another military dictatorship.

Members of Islamic political parties also feared United States intervention. Many felt that the repression they and others suffered under Suharto in the 1970s and 1980s was in part due to United States influence. Given the repeated pointing of fingers at Indonesia after the 11 September 2001 attack, exemplified by Lee Kuan Yew's description of the country as a 'terrorists' haven', Indonesian Muslims feared that the next intervention was likely to be directed at them. And, indeed, in an official State Department strategy statement concerning the War on Terror, released only briefly, soon after 11 September, the United States proposed direct military intervention in places like Afghanistan or Iraq, and 'more *indirect* measures in Indonesia and countries with similar problems' (US State Department website, 2002).

As far as Indonesian observers are concerned, this was not just idle talk. Rumour has it that is was no coincidence that Laskar Jihad leader, Ja'far Umar Thalib, was arrested for inciting conflict between Muslims and Christians in Sulawesi on 4May 2002. The arrest came just two days before US Ambassador Ralph Boyce was to visit this strife-torn region and while Defense Secretary Donald Rumsfeld was trying to convince the United States Congress that ties with and financial aid for the Indonesian military should be resumed, as soon as possible, regardless of the military's participation in the East Timor massacre two years earlier (see *ICG* 2002). None of these events provides clear proof of US intentions in Indonesia, but many ordinary Indonesian observers feel quite certain that such events are evidence of a negative conspiratorial pattern.

Conspiracy theories are not confined to any specific sector of society. It must be emphasised, in particular, that educated modern Indonesians have long been aware of their place as pawns in global political games. And, regardless of whether they are Muslims or non-Muslims, right or left-wing, modernists or traditionalists, fundamentalists or moderates, this awareness has not made them fond of American foreign policy. My informants all tend to share fundamentally similar perceptions of the United States, although their views may range from reasonable suspicion to wild conspiracy theories, from measured criticism to mindless condemnation. And the issues that Indonesians consider in forming such views are by no means confined to politics, let alone religion. For example, many view with deep suspicion their country's economic dependence on the International Monetary Fund (IMF), the World Bank and the Paris Club of creditor nations (Lane 2002). Indeed, in 2001 many feared that their country was travelling along the same IMF-dictated path as Argentina, whose economy reached meltdown point on 5 September 2001.

All of these processes of opinion formation have to be considered carefully and in some detail if we wish to understand and disentangle Indonesian popular and government reactions to the US-led War on Terror and similar world political events. In the following I shall describe some of the responses I was able to observe in Java in September 2001 and over the following months and years.

First reactions: divine justice

My observations suggest that the Afghanistan war, and the War on Terror of which it is said to be the beginning, has aided Islamic hardliners in their battle for the hearts of Indonesian Muslims and may also be aiding hardliners in the nationalist camp. My conclusion draws on a study of reports, editorials and readers' letters in Indonesian and Javanese that appeared in the Javanese press or in the newsletters of various organisations at the time. I also draw on my countless conversations with ordinary Javanese and various stakeholders.

The 11 September incident, the first significant breach in the security of the United States mainland since 1812, was greeted with considerable glee in Java— in the press as well as in the streets. What perfunctory expressions of sympathy there were, on account of the innocent victims of the attacks, were drowned by lengthy and often quite savage accounts of what the American empire had done over many decades to deserve being 'struck in its vital organs by almighty Allah', as Bin Laden put it (Ali 2002:2). When the United States revealed its plan for a revenge strike on Afghanistan, there was a strong public outburst of solidarity with the Taliban, even from people who, in normal circumstances, would have hastened to distance themselves from the Taliban brand of Islam.

As the views of Islamic hardliners gained currency, Osama t-shirts with slogans such as 'he [Bin Laden] is my brother' became instantly fashionable in Java and were also sold in Bali, even in the tourist market. Much of the discourse in the media and in the streets at the time was anti-imperialist *schadenfreude* rather than a well-developed pro-Islamist discourse. In other words, the sentiments expressed were more political than religious.

As the United States retaliation in Afghanistan began there was a much broader outburst of public solidarity with the Taliban, and broader support for radical Islamic groups within Indonesia itself. What actions this solidarity with 'Muslim brothers' in Afghanistan called for were a matter of disagreement. The public debate became increasingly one-sided, however, because the opinions most widely publicised and sensationalised in the Indonesian mass media were those of a small minority of Islamic hardliners. Javanese newspapers did not necessarily endorse the activities of the Islamic right, which included demonstrations in all major Javanese cities, but, nevertheless, focused heavily on them. Few moderate Muslims, Hindus or Christians in Java dared to speak out against the powerful anti-American rhetoric put forward by the more radically-minded at that time, partly because the nationalists had mixed feelings themselves and did not manage to articulate a clear alternative position.

When some militant Islamic groups, including Laskar Jihad and the Front of Islamic Defenders (FPI), began to roam the streets enlisting Indonesian Muslims to join a 'holy war' against the 'American devil' and to issue threats of so-called 'sweepings' against foreign nationals, there continued to be a conspicuous lack of objection from the more moderate sectors of Javanese society. The Indonesian government, including President Megawati, was silenced or at least constrained by the powerful surge of public support for a new radical nationalism with a dominant Islamic flavour.

Few moderate Javanese Muslims spoke out publicly against the early tide of anti-Americanism; some feared being branded as traitors to the cause of Islam, others were perhaps temporarily moved to sympathy for other Muslims by the emotional hype in the media. Even when critical voices and balanced views became more commonly heard in private conversation, the dominant public voice of Indonesian Muslims, as heard in the Indonesian media, was still that of an Islamic hardline minority.

The most prominent expressions of moderate views at this early stage were found in the official statements of the Indonesian government—intended for an international audience. The government's attempts to calm the public and rein in extremists were half-hearted, however, and came too late to prevent a drop in tourism, foreign investment and the exchange rate. The Megawati government was silenced temporarily and was constrained more permanently by the powerful public appeal of Islamic rhetoric, even more so than the Suharto government was in the 1990s. The government was unable or unwilling to control even its own Islamic spokespeople. This became evident, when leaders of the state-sponsored Majelis Ulama Indonesia (MUI) joined the hardliners' call for a *jihad*. MUI later explained at length what they had and had not meant when they used the word *jihad*, but the damage was done.

The coalition government was also internally divided, and the events of 11 September 2001 made this all the more obvious. Hamzah Haz, the nation's Vice-President and leader of the mainstream Muslim United Development Party (PPP), undermined Megawati's promise of support to President Bush, even while she was visiting Washington in September 2001. Also, at the forefront of the 2002 general assembly (MPR) meeting, Hamzah stirred up the age-old debate on the Jakarta Charter which had been rejected at the time of Indonesian independence (see also Platzdasch 2001), by supporting in principle the introduction of Islamic law (*syariah*), which some groups wanted to use as a constitutional foundation for creating an Islamic Indonesian state. Hamzah claimed that the imposition of *syariah* '[would] not adversely affect non-Muslims in Indonesia'. He increased the stakes further by visiting Laskar Jihad leader Umar Thalib in prison and by holding a meeting with the now notorious Abu Bakar Ba'asyir, the leader of the militant Majelis Mujahedin Indonesia and Afghanistan veteran who had by that time been accused of Al-Qaeda links (*Straits Times* 2002). Hamzah was also involved in efforts to consolidate Indonesia's numerous Islamic splinter parties into a single anti-secular alliance in advance of the 2004 elections. So much for the benefit the War on Terror delivered to the hawks of religious politics in Indonesia.

Complacency and the effects of this internal division characterised the response of the Indonesian government not only to the international War on Terror, but also to religiously inspired acts of terrorism at home. In 2001 arrests of known domestic militants were few, selective and mostly extrajudicial. The FPI, for example, was allowed to launch dozens of violent attacks in Jakarta alone with almost complete impunity. And there were many other incidents during the early *reformasi* years that bore testimony to an increase in religious persecution, acts of terrorism, vigilante killings, extortion rackets and paramilitary groups in Indonesia, all of which are part of a broader milieu of political and economic violence. The result was a pervasive climate of fear wherein, building on the foundation of a religious rhetoric of social identity, a mere rumour could suffice to drive a wedge between people and incite violence. In short, it was a climate in which both domestic political manipulation and foreign intervention were widely regarded as distinct possibilities.

Subsequent reactions: dealing with domestic terrorism

Javanese society has long been cited as the model case of a softer, Southeast Asian brand of Islam. This image is now in need of some adjustment, but in a way it still seemed true in late 2001. Although religious tolerance and political moderation had gradually decreased in Java, it still did not seem as if popular reactions to the war in Afghanistan would reach a point where threats of sweepings against foreigners, for example, would actually be carried out. When it did seem as if violent actions were imminent on a number of occasions, especially in Solo on 23 September 2001, mainstream Islamic organisations including Mohammadiyah quickly condemned the incident. The government adjusted its strategy too, in that they finally did crack down on some of the most militant organisations in early December 2001 (for example in Ngawi, where PDI-P affiliated racketeers had clashed with Laskar Jihad).

The arguments put forward by speakers of government and non-government organisations in favour of political moderation, however, were insincere. For example, rather than arguing against the sweepings of foreign tourists and expatriates on the moral grounds that these were innocent travellers, many moderates highlighted the fact that a massive flight of foreign capital would follow any such attack and that this would adversely affect the Indonesian economy. In short, the discourse was one of economic rationality rather than friendship or moral principle (cf Ravenhill 2002).

The government's weak efforts to crack down on prominent militant leaders also gave cause for concern at the time. The chairman of the paramilitary FPI, Habib Riziek Shihab, for example, arrogantly refused to come in for questioning and the police were afraid to arrest him at first, following a number of open threats against them. It was also worrying that little was done to investigate radical elements in Darul Islam, a longstanding radical Muslim organisation whose spokesman, Al Chaidar, publicly stated that one of its splinter factions was behind bomb attacks on an Australian International School in South Jakarta in November 2001, as well as the Petra Protestant Church bombing in North Jakarta.

Six months later, by mid 2002, the situation had changed again. The media and the public lost interest in Afghanistan, Islamic radicals became a little less willing to broadcast their views for fear that someone could be watching after all, and moderate Muslims from many different organisations had had time to reflect on popular reactions in those first two months after 11 September. Moderates made good use of that time by raising and publicly debating many important issues concerning the role of Islam in modern life, in Indonesian politics and in the world at large. Nevertheless, some of the damage could not be undone.

What remained as a more permanent and dangerous legacy was a new sense that Islamic sensitivities among an increasing number of fundamentalist-leaning Indonesians are not to be ignored by anyone wishing to survive in Indonesia's domestic political scene. Megawati's government certainly recognised the mood of the day and exercised maximum restraint in dealing with Islamic radicalism. Popular fears of a military comeback in the name of the War on Terror proved incorrect. Alas, with the benefit of hindsight, we now know that in trying to find the right balance in this difficult situation, the Indonesian government erred on the side of caution.

The Bali attack: merely a change of scale?

The 12 October 2002 bomb attack in Kuta, Bali, showed that the response of Indonesian society and government to the gradual escalation of acts of political violence had not been firm enough to discourage the perpetrators of this attack of terrorism or others like them. I would argue that the attack became a major turning point in Indonesian popular opinion and politics.

It cannot be denied that the response to the Bali attack was swift. The Indonesian police is to be commended for arresting most of the people immediately involved in the bombing within a relatively short time, partly because of a new willingness to accept the help of foreign colleagues and institutions. At the same time, however, the government still showed a lack of political will to authorise the pursuit of terrorists on a broader scale, that is, the arrest of all active members of the organisations involved in the attack regardless of whether they were individually involved in this particular event or not. The reason for this enduring caution was that the change in popular opinion after Bali, though it was significant, was not deep enough to support more sweeping government action against religious extremism. This strategy persists, and is evident, for example, in the way the 2009 Marriott and Ritz Carlton Hotel bombing in Jakarta was handled.

Indonesians after the Bali attack were no longer be able to deny the existence of terrorist networks in their midst who were willing to kill. For many, whether terrorist action is legitimate and, if so, under what circumstances, are still very much open questions. If these questions are discussed in abstract terms— independent of the negative practical impact that acts of terror have had on Indonesia's tourism industry and foreign investment prospects—many people privately entertain the view that under some circumstances terrorist attacks are a perfectly legitimate, even a heroic form of warfare. Most of the people I have spoken with nonetheless despise the targeting of innocent civilians. In short, the battle for Indonesian hearts and minds continues.

Just to give one small example. Ulil Abshar-Abdalla, outspoken founder of the moderate Islamic group Jaringan Islam Liberal, was made a target by a group of East Javanese religious leaders (*ulama*) in response to an openly critical appraisal of narrowly literalist and militant forms of Islam he published in *Kompas* in 2003. The group of *ulama* issued a *fatwa* saying that he should be killed. Although few public commentators had any sympathy for this ultra-defensive stance, few were willing to condemn the *fatwa* as an incitement to murder. In short, even after the Bali terrorist attack there has been a remarkable degree of tolerance of fundamentalism. Acts like the issue of this *fatwa*, which effectively aim to intimidate Islamic moderates, are still permitted to take place. It is not surprising, therefore, that strong moderate voices continue to be in short supply in the public domain.

With a further attack on a McDonald's restaurant in Makassar on 5 December 2002, the Marriott Hotel bombing in Jakarta on 5 August 2003, and a second Bali bombing in 2003, it seems that even the more vehement pursuit of terrorism that began in the wake of the 2002 Bali bombing will not be enough to eliminate the possibility of further attacks. The underlying problems and the main restraints on government action remain the same—first, there is considerable public support for a hard-line response to the actual or suspected imperialist agenda of the West, and second, there are fears that any large-scale crackdown on militant Islam would lead to civil war, bringing the military back into the foreground and thus jeopardising Indonesia's hard-won chance for democracy. Even under the current president, former army general Susilo Bambang Yudhoyono, the government's response has continued to accommodate public sentiment driven by local interpretations of world political events.

The unilateral American attack on Iraq in March 2003 and the subsequent failure to find evidence of weapons of mass destruction in Iraq has tended to confirm both the reasonable and the unreasonable suspicions that many ordinary Indonesians have about the foreign policies of the United States and its allies. The invasion and occupation of Iraq has played into the hands of militant Islamic organisations and has once again decreased the present government's ability to convince the public of the need for Indonesia to crack down on international and domestic terrorism.

Swings in public opinion in Indonesia, in response to the tides of terrorism and of the War on Terror, are, of course, not unique. Similar reactions can be seen in Muslim majority countries elsewhere in Asia and in the Middle East. Such swings can be expected to continue. On a more hopeful note, however, I have observed a very strong increase in reflexivity among the many Indonesians I have conversed with since 2001. People from all walks of life are now quite thoughtful in their reflections about Islam, politics and terrorism, and have become more knowledgeable, more cautious, and less prone to drawing premature conclusions. In general, public debate in the mass media is now more refined and sophisticated, and fewer people are willing to produce or listen to simplistic, hate-filled anti-Western propaganda. In my opinion, if acts of terror continue and the government responds firmly without over-reacting, terrorism will gradually defeat itself by alienating public sentiment. At the same time, if the War on [Islamic] Terror continues, and continues in a unilateral spirit, then, for the foreseeable future, terrorists will be produced in Indonesia faster than they can be found and arrested. Recent political changes in the US and Australia give room for some hope that the less desirable of the two options can be avoided.

Notes

1 My research in Java and, earlier, in Bali has been generously supported by a succession of ARC grants and fellowships, and, since 2006, by a Senior Research Fellowship from Monash University.

chapter eight

Disdained but indispensable: political parties in post-Suharto Indonesia

Dirk Tomsa

At first sight, writing about Indonesian political parties under the theme 'reasons for hope' may seem like a tough proposition. No matter what kind of resources I consulted in preparing this chapter, the judgement on the performance of the people's representatives was almost inevitably negative. The Indonesian media, to begin with, has over the last few years produced dozens, if not hundreds, of articles that are scathingly critical of the parties, mainly because of their seemingly endless internal squabbling, their poor parliamentary track record and, of course, the high levels of corruption within the parties. Similarly, public opinion polls throughout the last ten years have, with worrisome consistency, listed political parties among the least trusted political actors and institutions in the country. Last, but not least, numerous academic scholars, including myself, have repeatedly pointed out that most Indonesian parties have made little progress towards institutionalisation since the beginning of the reform era and have, therefore, directly contributed to the somewhat protracted character of Indonesia's democratic transition. And yet, in the midst of all these gloomy assessments of the parties there is, I believe, some reason for hope.

While this chapter is not designed to refute or deny the validity of the overall consensus that seems to have emerged in the literature on Indonesian parties—on the contrary, it will actually reiterate many of the criticisms levelled at the parties in the past—it will point out that none of their numerous weaknesses have actually reached such severe levels that they could have derailed the overall direction of Indonesia's democratisation process. As a matter of fact, ten years after the fall of Suharto, Indonesia's young democracy can look back on a number of remarkable achievements. Yet, these achievements may count for little if no further efforts are undertaken to address the many challenges that remain. Parties will need to do more if they are to play a constructive role in enhancing political accountability and efficiency of governance in Indonesia.

This chapter will develop an argument that highlights the parties' current weaknesses and the necessity to overcome at least some of them. It will argue that, even though they have, so far, contributed fairly little to Indonesia's democratisation process, political parties are indispensable for the country's political future. Even though the remarks in this chapter do not exactly ooze with optimism, they reject notions that parties will soon become redundant in the increasingly personalised politics of post-Suharto Indonesia. If the country is to further consolidate its young democracy, it will need to strengthen its parties, not weaken them.

Democratisation theory and political parties

Conventional democratisation theory maintains that political parties should play a vital role in the consolidation of emerging democracies. Linz and Stepan (1996), for example, described them as a critical element of the so-called 'political society', one of five arenas in which the process of consolidation is played out. Similarly, Merkel (1998:50) argued that 'ideology, structure and behaviour of the parties are…of utmost importance for the survival or breakdown of young democracies'. And according to Randall (2006), parties are crucial, not least because they are the only organisations that can provide effective opposition, which is extremely important for the proper functioning of parliament and the overall consolidation of democracy.

The importance of parties is grounded in their strategic position at the intermediate level between state and society. Like no other political organisations, parties can, if they perform their duties well, link ordinary people to the government and the legislature. In many Western countries, parties are key to the stability and legitimacy of modern democracy as they are instrumental not only in the aggregation and representation of competing societal interests, but also in the recruitment of new personnel into political decision-making processes and in the crafting and implementation of policy agendas (Gunther & Diamond 2001). In short, parties are indispensable for the functioning of modern democracy.

In many developing countries, democratic structures are only just emerging and parties are often ill-equipped to fulfil many of the functions listed above. Adverse socioeconomic circumstances, coupled with the manifold legacies of colonialism and long periods of post-colonial authoritarianism, have significantly impeded the development of political parties (Randall 2006). It should, therefore, not be surprising that many parties in democratising countries display, as Carothers (2006:8) stated, 'a tendency toward leader-centrism, top-down organisational management, non-transparent and often highly personalistic financing, relentless electoralism, and ideological vagueness.' In other words, they are weakly institutionalised.

In the scholarly literature there is broad consensus that low levels of party institutionalisation tend to have negative implications for the institutionalisation of the overall party system and, ultimately, for democratic consolidation (Randall & Svåsand 2002a; Mainwaring 1999). Parties that exhibit the abovementioned characteristics are, for example, unlikely to properly represent the interests of their voters, as they will prioritise self-interest over citizens' interests. They are also unlikely to provide meaningful political education to voters, since they are merely interested in getting votes, rather than socialising people into the values and procedures of democratic politics (Carothers 2006:11–12). On a broader scale, poorly institutionalised parties often directly contribute to the weakening of public trust in politics in general. Thus, it is important to note that, despite the general consensus about the indispensability of parties, it cannot simply be assumed 'that parties are functional for democracy or its consolidation; on the contrary, it may be expected that in some circumstances they are part of the problem' (Randall & Svåsand 2002b:4).

Party	% of votes won		gain/loss
	1999	2004	
Partai Golkar	22.44	21.58	-0.86
Partai Demokrasi Indonesia Perjuangan (PDI-P)	33.74	18.53	-15.21
Partai Kebangkitan Bangsa (PKB)	12.61	10.57	-2.04
Partai Persatuan Pembangunan (PPP)	10.71	8.15	-2.56
Partai Demokrat (PD)	–	7.45	+7.45
Partai Keadilan Sejahtera (PKS)	1.36	7.34	+5.98
Partai Amanat Nasional (PAN)	7.12	6.44	-0.68

Source: Ananta, Arifin & Suryadinata (2005:14–22).

The remainder of the chapter will leave little doubt that, in Indonesia, parties are indeed part of the problem. Towards the end of the chapter, however, it should also become clear that there is at least some reason for hope that developments in Indonesian party politics might at least not get worse than they have been since 1998. Using some benchmark criteria of party institutionalisation theory developed by Randall and Svåsand (2001; 2002a) as a rough structural framework, the following paragraphs will outline some of the most pressing weaknesses of Indonesia's political parties. The chapter will then move on to discuss some of the positive aspects of the parties' performance before concluding with some tentative remarks about the future of Indonesian party politics. The analysis will focus on the seven biggest parties in Indonesia, each of which reached more than 5% of votes in one or both of the 1999 and 2004 elections.[1]

The organisational dimension

At first sight, it seems as if territorial representation should be the least of the parties' worries. If, for example, we take documents submitted to the electoral commission, Komisi Pemilihan Umum or attendances of regional delegates at national party congresses as guidelines of geographic depth, one can get the impression that all of the seven big parties have well-established nationwide organisational infrastructures. Indeed, on paper most of the big parties do have provincial and district offices, even in the remotest areas of the sprawling archipelago. Naked figures of party offices, however, are misleading. Like their counterparts in other democratising countries, Indonesian parties, too, are overwhelmingly electoralist. In organisational terms, that means that party offices at the local level are often deserted outside election times. Moreover, the few executives that maintain the appearance of a local party presence are rarely professional politicians who are able to communicate complex political problems and their solutions to the people at the grassroots. With recruitment strategies and training programs usually poorly developed or nonexistent, most parties suffer from a serious lack of competent human resources. In the run-up to the 2004 legislative elections, this lack of professional personnel was reflected in comparatively large numbers of proposed candidates who failed to fulfil basic medical or educational requirements prescribed in the election law (Tomsa 2008).

Most affected by this problem are parties whose members are recruited primarily from the lower segments of society, especially PPP, PKB and PDI-P. At the other end of the spectrum, Golkar can still fall back on a fairly large pool of experienced and reasonably well-educated cadres who have helped the party of the former regime maintain an image of relative professionalism. Arguably, the only other party that has also been able to develop an aura of professionalism—though on a much smaller scale—is PKS. Sometimes regarded as the best-organised party in Indonesia, PKS owes its reputation mainly to its unmatched internal discipline and its predominantly well-educated cadres in the top ranks of the party hierarchy.

It is, however, not only the territorial depth and the professionalism of its cadres that determine a party's organisational strength, or 'systemness', as some scholars have called it (Panebianco 1988, Randall & Svåsand 2002a). The structure of leadership, the effectiveness and stability of internal rules and regulations, and the party's ability to access a diverse range of financial resources all have an impact on a party's degree of organisation as well. And arguably, it is in these aspects of party organisation that many Indonesian parties have particularly serious problems.

With regards to leadership, few parties, if any, have so far found the right balance between strong leadership and an engaged and participatory membership base. In some parties, charismatic leaders have been so overwhelmingly dominant within the internal power structure that neither ordinary members nor top-ranking party officials in the central leadership boards have had a chance to decisively influence the overall direction of the party. PDI-P under Megawati, PKB under Abdurrahman Wahid, and PAN under Amien Rais (until 2005)[2] are the most prominent examples in this regard. Similarly, PD is so dependent on its figure head Susilo Bambang Yudhoyono (SBY) that it is unlikely that the party will ever make decisions against its patron, even though the incumbent President is not even a formal member of the leadership board.

In contrast to PDI-P, PKB and PAN, parties like PPP and Golkar have long suffered from rather weak leadership. Between 1998 and 2004 Golkar was chaired by Akbar Tandjung, an experienced and astute but dull career politician whose time at the helm of the party was overshadowed by corruption allegations and consistent internal opposition against his leadership. Given these weaknesses, his chairmanship was intrinsically linked to his ability to maintain intricate patronage networks and ensure access to governmental power for his many clients in and outside the party. Once he miscalculated crucial shifts in the power balance in Jakarta in 2004, he was almost ousted by a disappointed party base (Tomsa 2006). Akbar's successor as chairman, the nation's Vice-President Jusuf Kalla, has so far elicited little open resistance to his leadership, but, just like his predecessor, Kalla will ultimately depend on his ability to keep Golkar inside and not outside the corridors of power.

The peculiar power structures in Indonesia's parties have given rise to widespread factionalism. Since patronage rather than merit usually decides a cadre's position in the party hierarchy, dissatisfaction, splits and defections are commonplace. As a matter of fact, over the last ten years all major parties have been affected by the emergence of splinter groups. Almost invariably, these groups call themselves 'reformist', but in the vast majority of cases their rhetoric does not match their actions. In fact, most splinter groups that have been established over the years have employed the very same style of politics they ostensibly set out to displace.

Where patronage and factionalism reign supreme, written rules and regulations have little influence on actors' expectations and actions. Accordingly, party constitutions and standing orders often exist only on paper with little chance of becoming routinised. This problem is further aggravated in many parties by the absence of regular influxes of financial resources. Only PKS is believed to generate at least some of its funding from membership dues, whereas all other parties are characterised by opaque and poorly institutionalised mechanisms of financial administration. External donations and irregular dues collected from parliamentarians and top cadres still make up the bulk of the parties' operating budgets, especially after the government drastically cut state subsidies to parties in 2005. As Mietzner (2007) has argued, this policy change, presumably intended to strengthen the parties by reducing their dependence on the state, has had largely negative effects on the parties as the decline in revenues from the state has further heightened the ever-increasing influence of big business money in Indonesian party politics (Sugiarto 2006).

Decisional autonomy

The combination of personalistic party structures based on patronage and a lack of regular and diversified funding not only weakens the organisational routine of a party, but also compromises its decisional autonomy as a collective political actor. Two closely intertwined problems seem to be of particular significance here. First, in Indonesia, decision-making processes within political parties are, more often than not, determined by financial concerns rather than policy considerations, or at least strongly influenced by them. Second, these decision-making processes are often highly oligarchic, leaving little or no room for the grassroots to be involved in important policy or personnel decisions.

Of course, a tendency towards oligarchy is an almost natural phenomenon in any large social organisation (Michels 1959)—not only in political parties and certainly not only in Indonesian parties. In order to operate successfully, big organisations simply have to concentrate the authority to make important decisions at the top of their organisational infrastructure. However, in Indonesia patterns of oligarchic party politics do appear to be inherently problematic, mainly because they are often compounded by the absence of accountability mechanisms and consultation processes between the party elite and the grassroots. Almost all parties are at fault here, but, arguably, those with strong and charismatic leaders are particularly neglectful towards the party organisation.

One party that at least for a limited time opened up new participatory avenues for its lower-ranking cadres is Golkar, which, in the run-up to the 2004 presidential election, experimented with an American-style convention to select its presidential candidate. Although the main motivation behind the decision to hold a convention was certainly not to empower the party's regional cadres, but rather to consolidate power in the hands of then party leader Akbar Tandjung (Tomsa 2006), the convention quickly developed its own dynamics and eventually produced a completely unexpected result which to a large extent was due precisely to the inclusion of the party grassroots in the convention.[3]

Having received plenty of praise for holding the presidential convention, Golkar adopted similar mechanisms to nominate its candidates in the massive wave of direct gubernatorial, mayoral and district head elections (*pemilihan kepala daerah*, or *pilkada*) that began in 2005. Other parties soon emulated Golkar's model, often commending themselves for introducing innovative democratic mechanisms into their decision-making procedures. But the more *pilkada* were held, the more apparent it became that the candidates running in these elections often owed their nomination not to their organisational merits or their persuasive program, but mainly to their brimming bank accounts. In other words, the conventions held by many local party chapters in the run-up to a *pilkada* were not nearly as democratic as local party bosses would try to make their followers believe. As a matter of fact, the final nod for the nomination was often given to those candidates who had offered the largest amount of money to the local party board. Thus, in many of these convention processes the decisional autonomy of the party as a collective actor was severely compromised by the prevalence of informal financial contributions aimed at bending or at least influencing existing modes of decision-making.[4]

Apart from problems with oligarchic elites and money politics, some parties are also restricted in their decisional autonomy by their close ties with supporting social mass organisations. PAN is one party that is of concern here because of its close relations with Muhammadiyah, but the party's central board is not exclusively occupied by Muhammadiyah officials so that it is at least formally independent. PKB, however, is clearly not entirely autonomous in its decision-making procedures as its organisational infrastructure partly overlaps with that of its support organisation Nahdlatul Ulama (NU). The two organisations were so closely intertwined, especially in the first six or seven years of the *reformasi* era, that it was basically impossible for PKB as a party to act against the interests of NU. Thus, PKB was restricted not only in its autonomy because of its personalistic leadership structure under Abdurrahman Wahid, but also because of its organisational dependence on NU. More recently, the relationship between the party and the mass organisation has become increasingly complex as factional frictions and defections have taken their toll on PKB's organisational coherence.

Value infusion

In addition to accusations of poorly developed party infrastructures, a lack of professionalism and widespread corruption, Indonesia's parties are also frequently criticised for their lack of programmatic depth. Such 'ideological vagueness' (Carothers 2006:8), however, is, once again, hardly a problem that is peculiar to Indonesia only. On the contrary, as numerous observers have noted, there is a clearly discernible global trend towards broad-based electoralist parties without sophisticated platforms, so Indonesia is by no means alone in this regard. But, global trends aside, there is another Indonesia-specific reason why we should hardly be surprised about the programmatic shallowness of most Indonesian parties, and that is the country's long history of de-politicisation and de-ideologisation during the New Order.

The spectrum of Indonesia's current parties emerged out of an ideological void that was deliberately created by a regime that regarded any kind of political or religious ideology as divisive. In many ways, Golkar was an archetypical product of this era. Established in 1964, it developed into a de facto regime party in the 1970s and 1980s, even though the Suharto government officially denied that it was a political party. Significantly, Golkar's *raison d'être* during the New Order was not to represent the people, but rather to serve the interests of the developing state.[5] To do so, a fully-fledged ideological foundation was neither necessary nor desired.

As a matter of fact, the lack of political competition during the New Order made it essentially pointless for Golkar to shape a value-based ideology. The authoritarian nature of the state was sufficient to ensure that voters did not need to be wooed with sophisticated political ideas. With the advent of the reform era in 1998, however, things changed. Suddenly confronted with an unprecedented number of electoral rivals, Golkar initially found it difficult to redefine its corporate identity. While some elements inside the party argued in favour of an internal debate about how Golkar could develop a more convincing ideological foundation, others—and it seems that this latter group was by far in the majority within the party—insisted that Golkar's ideology of not having an ideology is precious and should continue to form the basic rationale of the party. Not surprisingly then, Golkar today remains a party that largely fits the bill of 'ideological vagueness', even though traces of a distinctly pluralist-nationalist outlook may be discernible in its program.

Where strong political values are absent, parties often try to use the appeal of charismatic leaders to attract voters. Golkar does not fall into this category,[6] but many other Indonesian parties do. The most blatantly personalistic party is arguably PD, which relies almost entirely on the charismatic appeal of a single individual, namely incumbent President Susilo Bambang Yudhoyono. Although the former general's active involvement in the party's day-to-day affairs has been practically nil, PD has been remarkably adroit at exploiting the President's loose affiliation with the party—he sponsored the establishment of the party for his presidential ambitions and is now chairman of its Advisory Council—to solidify its position in the Indonesian party system.

To rely almost entirely on the appeal of a single individual, however, is a risky strategy for any party that intends to become institutionalised in the long term. And, given that the Indonesian constitution prescribes a maximum of two consecutive terms for a President, it is clear that PD will eventually be forced to develop some sort of corporate identity beyond the incumbent President's popular appeal. Moreover, it may be noteworthy that while SBY remains popular right now, there is no guarantee whatsoever that this will remain the case indefinitely.

If PD's prospects to become a party that is 'valuable in and of itself' (Panebianco 1988:53) appear bleak unless it manages to routinise SBY's charisma, other parties that also rely heavily on the mass appeal of their leaders seem to be slightly better positioned. PDI-P and PKB, for instance, are both led by charismatic leaders (Megawati Sukarnoputri and Abdurrahman Wahid respectively), as was PAN until Amien Rais relinquished formal control of the party in 2005. What distinguishes these parties from PD, however, is their perceived rootedness in fairly clearly-defined sociocultural and socioeconomic milieus, commonly referred to as *aliran* structures (King 2003; Baswedan 2004; Tan 2004; Ufen 2006). Some scholars argue that this rootedness endows them with tangible political values that not only link them with similarly oriented parties in the 1950s (PDI-P with Partai Nasional Indonesia, PKB with NU, PAN with Masyumi), but also ensure their survival long after their current leaders will have left the scene. Accordingly, PDI-P is said to represent secular-nationalist values, PKB is the mouthpiece of traditionalist Islam, and PAN represents values commonly associated with modernist Islam.

There is certainly little doubt that the sociocultural and socioeconomic profiles of today's PDI-P, PKB and PAN constituencies are similar to those of the corresponding parties of the 1950s. To what extent, however, the present-day parties are really and thoroughly infused with those values their spiritual predecessors fought so fervently for remains as debated as the question of the extent to which these alleged values influence voting behaviour today. Those who believe that *aliran* approaches continue to have enduring explanatory relevance argue that the decisions people make at the ballot box are directly determined by their social milieu. Where today's parties fail to formulate compelling policy platforms—so the argument goes—voters base their decisions about their electoral preferences on their understanding of long-established political traditions that reach back to the 1950s, when the *aliran* structures were shaped and irrevocably linked to political parties.

Critics of the *aliran* approach agree with many of the abovementioned arguments, but they disagree about the relative importance of such frozen *aliran* structures for determining present-day electoral behaviour. Liddle and Mujani (2000), for example, wrote in an influential paper about the 1999 elections that religious affiliations and other social cleavages are only secondary factors for the development of voting preferences. According to the authors, it is not *aliran* structures but a strong emotional attachment to charismatic national leaders that primarily shapes people's party choices. Since the 2004 elections, Liddle and Mujani's argument has gained more weight as the importance of *aliran* structures appears to have declined. But the ultimate answer to the question of what is the single most important factor in determining the voting behaviour of supporters of PDI-P, PKB and PAN may only be found after Megawati, Abdurrahman Wahid and Amien Rais will have left the political stage completely.

PDI-P, PKB and PAN may be termed 'hybrid parties' because they combine the appeal of charismatic leaders with the values of old-established social streams. In contrast to this, the Islamist PKS almost exclusively links its identity to a set of religious core values that serve as the party's 'spirit'.[7] Emerging out of student activist circles at the beginning of the post-Suharto era, this party deliberately avoided looking back to the past in its search for values. Instead, its leaders recognised the potential for Islam to be redefined as a political force in accordance with the changing political and social circumstances in Indonesia. While the 1999 election came too soon for this young party, in 2004 it won more than 7% of the vote. For a moment it seemed as if PKS might have lifted Islamic politics in Indonesia into a new dimension because the party did not rely on labels such as traditionalism or modernism. Instead, it had endeavoured to develop its own Islamic identity. This identity is based on the party's self-perception as a *dakwah* party and its firm commitment to purity and clean government. Although other parties like PPP and a number of smaller parties also claim to represent the interests of Islam, one may argue that PKS is the only big party that has really incorporated the values of Islam into its political actions, rather than merely using Islam as a label for political purposes. That said, it should also be noted that some of the party's recent political manoeuvres during regional elections have cast serious doubts on the ultimate ability of PKS to resist the temptations of power.

Reification

So far this chapter has addressed some of the major problems often identified in discussions about Indonesian political parties. The focus has been on issues like weak organisational infrastructures, oligarchic decision-making processes, corruption and ideological vagueness. To varying extents, all these factors reflect internal problems within the parties.[8] Some political scientists, however, argue that, in order for political parties to institutionalise, they need not only to overcome the various aforementioned problems but also to become externally institutionalised or, as Janda (1980) put it, reified in the people's imagination.

This process of reification is an important indicator of whether a party is able to survive its founder and eventually become a household name in the public consciousness, regardless of its momentary leader. The problem here, of course, is that most Indonesian parties have not yet, or have only recently, experienced a change of leadership, so it seems somewhat unreasonable and premature to assess these criteria of party institutionalisation. However, early survey data about levels of name recognition indicate that public awareness of the major political parties is already reasonably high, even though there are significant discrepancies between the levels of name recognition for Golkar and PDI-P on the one hand (around 90%) and PKS on the other (just under 50%).[9] The gap confirms Randall and Svåsand's (2002a) statement that reification is first and foremost 'a function of longevity'. At the same time, it also shows that media exposure contributes greatly to a party's chances to become or remain reified, as the two biggest parties have received far more media coverage in the last ten years than the relatively new PKS. In the case of Golkar, media exposure has in fact played a vital role, not only in helping the former regime party to remain reified after the fall of Suharto, but also in reshaping its tarnished image and repositioning itself in the post-authoritarian party system (Tomsa 2007).

So, why is there reason for hope?

This brief analysis of the state of Indonesia's parties through the lens of some institutionalisation criteria suggests that much of the criticism levelled at the parties in recent years is indeed justified. Indonesian parties do suffer from a lot of problems and these problems have severely limited their ability to properly fulfil their functions as the people's representatives. In parliament, lack of professionalism, organisational incoherence and allegations of corruption have prevented the parties from passing many laws that were scheduled for discussion. Outside parliament, organisational shallowness and a lack of genuine political values have hindered many parties from formulating policy concepts or providing meaningful political education. In the words of Carothers (2006:175),

Indonesia's main political parties remain almost archetypical embodiments of the standard lament about parties—they are intensely leader-centric organisations dominated by a small circle of elite politicians who hold onto their positions atop parties seemingly indefinitely, are immersed in patronage politics, and who are far more devoted to political intrigues in the capital than the prosaic work of trying to listen to and represent a base of constituents.

And yet, despite the parties' poor track records, Indonesia's democratisation process has leapt many hurdles in the last ten years, and it is probably fair to say that at least some of these achievements can be linked, in one way or another, to the performance of the parties. The remaining paragraphs will highlight some of these achievements and conclude by arguing that the best way to further strengthen Indonesia's young democracy is to further strengthen the role of the political parties.

Arguably, one of the key achievements of Indonesia's democratisation process is that it has taken place without the emergence of radical or revisionist political parties that actively seek to undermine the country's young democracy. The major parties deserve some credit for this for two reasons. Firstly, they have, despite their manifold weaknesses, apparently performed well enough not to trigger so much popular discontent that a radical party, should it be established, would have a reasonable chance for success. The miserable performance of the Concern for the Nation Functional Party, Partai Karya Peduli Bangsa in the 2004 elections confirmed that, while they may be unhappy with their parties, Indonesians still prefer poorly-performing democratic parties to a party that openly glorified the authoritarianism of the New Order.

Secondly, the parties have, after prolonged and frequently-criticised negotiations in parliament, produced laws that make it difficult for potentially dangerous parties to be formed. In other words, they have created institutional arrangements that are designed to sustain the democratic system. Although every party involved in the deliberations naturally sought to defend its own interests, the various measures of political engineering taken by Indonesia's lawmakers have helped shape Indonesia's democratisation process. In the run-up to the 2009 legislative and presidential elections, no powerful social forces hostile to democracy were in sight,[10] leaving democracy, if only in its minimalist, electoral variant, as 'the only game in town'.

Another point worth mentioning may be that the parties have helped create laws that are designed to foster co-operation and reduce conflict. In a country like Indonesia, where the transition to democracy was accompanied by large-scale separatist and communal violence, this is an achievement that should definitely be emphasised. The 'co-operative spirit' is particularly evident in the laws for the presidential elections and the *pilkada*, which encourage candidates to team up with running mates who appeal to a different kind of constituency. In many ways, these laws have helped reduce the chances for radical candidates to contest elections, let alone win them.

The road ahead

Highlighting the positive effects of some of the most important political laws that have been deliberated by Indonesia's parties in the last decade may help us realise just how important parties can be for the consolidation of democracy in Indonesia. The parties' overall contribution may have been less than satisfactory so far, but they have had a significant impact on the shape of Indonesia's young democracy. No other political factor could have fulfilled this role, which is one of the reasons why parties are indeed indispensible, even in Indonesia. That said, the next step must be to fill shape with substance. Whether this huge step can be taken by the parties will depend to a large extent on their ability to redefine their place in an increasingly personalistic political system.[11]

There is little doubt that since the introduction of direct presidential elections and the *pilkada* the importance of parties in influencing and determining electoral outcomes has declined immensely. Several studies have shown that the once notoriously powerful 'party machines' have become basically irrelevant, especially in local elections (Buehler 2007, Buehler & Tan 2007), and there is little reason to believe that this trend may be reversed any time soon. On the contrary, the recent decision by the Constitutional Court to allow independent candidates to run in future local elections may even further erode the power of the parties.

Thus, Indonesian politics looks set to become even more personalistic than it already is. Parties will need to adapt to this trend, and one way—maybe the only promising way—to do so would be to finally initiate some credible steps towards improving their institutionalisation record. A quick look at the 2004 elections results should suffice to tell them that investing in the development of a reasonably solid and comprehensive party infrastructure would not only be appreciated by political scientists observing their performance, but could also confer direct results at the ballot box. Indeed, party institutionalisation matters not only in abstract academic discourses, but also right in a political competition, as was evident in 2004 when Golkar and PKS proved that institutionalisation can translate directly into votes. Golkar, on the one hand, returned to the top of the voting tally thanks to its far-reaching party apparatus, its huge reservoir of experienced and professional cadres and its high levels of name recognition. PKS, on the other hand, managed the second highest gains in the elections (after PD) because of its solid organisational base, its well-trained members and its credible political message of purity and political cleanliness.

In the years that followed the election, both parties failed to capitalise on their established strengths. Whereas PKS quickly alienated many of its supporters by pushing forward with highly controversial initiatives, such as the discriminative anti-pornography bill, Golkar fell back into complacency once the election of Jusuf Kalla as party chairman in December 2004 had secured ongoing access to lucrative patronage resources. Consequently, it seems as if much will remain the same after the 2009 elections. The good news is that this means more continuity and stability for the party system and, by implication, for Indonesia's democracy. Low-quality stability it may be, but, arguably, that is still better than no stability at all.

Notes

1 The 5% benchmark used here is higher than the actual electoral thresholds applied during the first three post-Suharto elections. It has been chosen here because it allows for clear differentiation between big and medium-sized parties, on the one hand, and small parties on the other hand. Generally speaking, it should be noted that the threshold regulation in Indonesia has been utterly ineffective, as it allows parties to take up seats in parliament even if they fail to reach the threshold (Mietzner 2006).

2 Amien relinquished the PAN chairmanship in 2005, but his successor, Soetrisno Bachir, is widely regarded as an Amien loyalist and many observers believe that Amien is still hugely influential behind the scenes in PAN.

3 Instead of Akbar Tandjung, party delegates from all over the country elected Retired General Wiranto as Golkar's presidential candidate. See Tomsa (2006) for more details on how Akbar lost the convention.

4 A similar phenomenon could also be observed during the 2004 legislative election where many parties were alleged to have sold the top ranks on their party lists to the highest bidder. The problem with this kind of procedure has been neatly summarised by Carothers (2006:12), who points out that '[p]arties that sell places on their candidate lists to wealthy political actors create members of parliament who think they need to steal sizeable amounts of money to make up for what they spent to get into power'.

5 As I have stressed elsewhere, during the New Order Golkar fulfilled exactly the functions which were once listed by Randall (1988) as typical for political parties in the developing world. Firstly and most importantly, it enhanced the regime's legitimacy by winning the regularly staged general elections (called *pesta demokrasi* in the regime's rhetoric). Secondly, the party helped the state to control society through its organisational infrastructure. And thirdly, Golkar functioned as the regime's recruitment pool for new political personnel (Tomsa 2008).

6 Golkar has long suffered from a lack of charismatic leaders. In the absence of both genuine political values and charismatic leaders, it relies heavily on its image as a government party that can deliver access to state patronage resources. Elsewhere, I have termed this basis of appeal 'ersatz values' to indicate how inferior this perceived party 'culture' is in comparison with genuine political values (Tomsa 2008).

7 Interview with Untung Wahono, 15 September 2004.

8 Randall and Svåsand (2002a) have conceptualised decisional autonomy as a specifically 'external dimension' of party institutionalisation, but arguably decisional autonomy also has implications for the internal functioning of a party. For more details, see Tomsa (2008).

9 Most other parties had levels of around 60% at the last available survey from 2005. See IFES (2005) for more details.

10 One may argue that Jema'ah Islamiyah is an exception here, but this terrorist organisation operates mostly outside the legal framework and its marginal status in Indonesian society rules it out as a serious threat to the democratic system.

11 Ironically, the growing trend towards personalism was facilitated by the parties themselves when their legislation paved the way for the introduction of direct presidential elections and the *pilkada*.

bibliography

Adam, Asvi Warman 2001 'Reconstructing, piece by piece' *Tempo* No. 04/II/2–8 October, www.tempointeraktif.com

Alamgir, Jalal 1997, 'Against the current: the survival of authoritarianism in Burma', *Pacific Affairs*, 70(3).

Ali, Tariq 2002, *The clash of fundamentalisms: crusades, jihads and modernity,* Verso, London.

Ananta, Aris, Evi Nurvidya Arifin and Leo Suryadinata 2005, *Emerging democracy in Indonesia*, Institute of Southeast Asian Studies, Singapore.

Anderson, Benedict R O'G 1972, *Java in a time of revolution: occupation and resistance, 1944–1946* Cornell University Press, Ithaca.

—— 1972, 'The idea of power in Javanese culture,' reprinted in Anderson Benedict R O'G 1990, *Language and power: exploring political cultures in Indonesia*, Cornell University Press, Ithaca.

Andrew, R, K Roesad and D Edwin 2005, 'Indonesia: the politics of inclusion', *Journal of Contemporary Asia*, 35(1).

Annual Report of the United States Commission on International Religious Freedom 2001, Washington, www.uscirf.gov.

Antlöv, Hans 2005, 'The social construction of power and authority in Java' in Hans Antlöv and Jörgen Hellman (eds), *The Java that never was: academic theories and political practices*, Lit, Munster.

Arblaster, Anthony 1994, *Democracy*, World View, Delhi.

Aretxaga, Begoña 2000 'A fictional reality: paramilitary death squads and the constructions of state terror in Spain', in JA Sluka (ed), *Death squad: the anthropology of state terror*, University of Pennsylvania Press, Philadelphia.

Aspinall, Edward 2005, *Opposing Soeharto: compromise, resistance, and regime change in Indonesia,* Stanford University Press, Stanford.

Atran, Scott 2005, 'In Indonesia, democracy isn't enough', editorial, *New York Times*, 5 October.

Aung-Thwin, Michael 2001, 'Parochial universalism, democracy Jihad and the Orientalist image of Burma: the new evangelism', *Pacific Affairs*, 74(4).

Barr, Michael 2004, *Cultural politics and Asian values: the tepid war*, Routledge, London.

Baswedan, Anies Rasyid 2004, 'Political Islam in Indonesia: present and future trajectory', *Asian Survey*, 44(5).

Benda, Harry 1958, *The crescent and the rising sun: Indonesian Islam under the Japanese Occupation 1942–1945*, W Van Hoeve, The Hague and Bandung.

Bhakti, Ikrar Nusa 2004. 'The transition to democracy in Indonesia: some outstanding problems' in Rolfe, Jim (ed), *The Asia Pacific: a region in transition*, Asia-Pacific Center for Security Studies, Honolulu.

Birks, Teresa 2006, *Neglected duty: providing comprehensive reparations to the Indonesian "1965 Victims" of State Persecution*, International Center for Transitional Justice, www.ictj.org/static/Asia/Indonesia/Indonesia1965.pdf

Bjornlund, Eric, William Liddle and Blair King 2005, 'Indonesia: democracy and governance assessment final report', prepared by Democracy International INC for the *United States Agency for International Development.*

Bourchier, David 1996, 'Lineages of organicist political thought in Indonesia', PhD thesis, Monash University, Clayton.

—— 1997, 'Totalitarianism and the "National Personality": recent controversy about the philosophical basis of the Indonesian State', in Schiller, Jim and Barbara Martin-Schiller (eds), *Imagining Indonesia*, Ohio University Center for International Studies, Athens.

Bourchier, David and Vedi R Hadiz 2003, *Indonesian politics and society: a reader*, Routledge, London.

Bubandt, Nils 2002, 'The dynamics of reasonable paranoia: rumours and riots in North Maluku 1999–2000', paper presented in the Anthropology Seminar Series, SAGES, University of Melbourne, 24 April 2002.

—— 2006, 'Sorcery, corruption, and the dangers of democracy in Indonesia', *Journal of the Royal Anthropological Institute* 12.

Buehler, Michael 2007, 'Local elite reconfiguration in post-New Order Indonesia: an analysis of the 2005 elections of district government heads', *Review for Indonesian and Malaysian Affairs*, 41(1).

Buehler, Michael and Paige Johnson Tan 2007, 'Party-candidate relationships in Indonesian local politics: a case study of the 2005 regional elections in Gowa, South Sulawesi Province', *Indonesia*, 84, October.

Carothers, Thomas 2006, *Confronting the weakest link: aiding political parties in new democracies*, Carnegie Endowment for International Peace, Washington.

Chauvel, Richard 2000, 'Indonesia's dead end in Papua,' *Age* Online, 26 December.

—— 2003, *The land of Papua and the Indonesian State: essays on West Papua*, Monash Asia Institute, Monash University Press.

Chauvel, Richard and Ikrar Nusa Bhakti 2004, *The Papua conflict: Jakarta's perceptions and policies*, East-West Center, Washington.

Diamond, Larry and Richard Gunther 2001, 'Types and functions of parties' in Diamond, Larry and Richard Gunther (eds), *Political parties and democracy*, Johns Hopkins University Press, Baltimore and London.

Drakeley, SM 2000, *Lubang Buaya: myth, misogyny and massacre*, Monash Asia Institute, Clayton.

Effendi, Tadjuddin Noer 1996, 'Demokrasi dalam perspektif budaya Batak' [Democracy in the Perspective of Batak's culture] in Najib, Muhammad (ed) 1996, *Demokrasi dalam perspektif budaya Nusantara* [*Democracy in the perspective of Indonesian cultures*], LKPSM, Yogyakarta.

Ellis, A 2005, 'One year after the elections: is democracy in Indonesia on course?' International IDEA, Strömsborg, Stockholm, 20 September.

Emmerson, Donald K 1976, *Indonesia's elite: political culture and cultural politics*, Cornell University Press, Ithaca.

Emmerson, Donald K 1999a, 'Exit and aftermath: the crisis of 1997–98', in Emmerson, Donald K (ed), *Indonesia beyond Suharto: polity, economy, society, transition* ME Sharpe, Armonk.

—— 1999b, 'Voting and violence: Indonesia and East Timor in 1999,' in Emmerson, Donald K (ed), *Indonesia beyond Suharto: polity, economy, society, transition* ME Sharpe, Armonk.

Fealy, Greg 2001, 'Inside the Laskar Jihad: an interview with the leader of a new, radical and militant sect', *Inside Indonesia*, Jan–Mar 2001.

Feillard, Andrée 1999, *NU vis-à-vis Negara: Pencarian Isi, Bentuk, dan Makna* [*NU vis-à-vis the State: the search for content, form, and meaning*], LKIS, Yogyakartach.

Feith, Herbert 1970, 'Introduction' in Feith, Herbert and Lance Castles (eds), *Indonesian political thinking, 1945–1965*, Cornell University Press, Ithaca.

Freedman, Amy L 2007, 'Consolidation or withering away of democracy? political changes in Thailand and Indonesia', *Asian Affairs* 33(4).

Fuadi, Ahmad, Seno Joko Suyono, Purwani Diyah Prabandari, Gita W Laksmini, Arief Kuswardono 2001, 'A list behind the bloodbath', *Tempo* magazine, 18 November.

Gazali, Effendi 2003, 'SARS dan politik nostalgi', *Kompas*, 27 December.

Geertz, Clifford 1960, *The religion of Java*, University of Chicago Press, Chicago.

Hadiz, Vedi 2000, 'Retrieving the past for the future? Indonesia and the New Order Legacy', *Southeast Asian Journal of Social Science* 28(2).

—— 2008, 'How far to meaningful democracy? What you see is what you get', Inside Indonesia 92.

Harijanto, Christian 2008, 'Why Indonesian people are losing interest in democracy?' *The Jakarta Post*, 4 February.

Hauswedell, Pieter Christian 1973, 'Sukarno: radical or conservative?' *Indonesia*, 15 April.

Hefner, Robert W 2000, *Civil Islam: Muslims and democratization in Indonesia* Princeton University Press, Princeton.

Heryanto, Ariel 1999, 'Where Communism never dies: violence, trauma and narration in the last Cold War Capitalist authoritarian state', *International Journal of Cultural Studies* 2(2).

—— 2006, *State-terrorism and identity politics in Indonesia: fatally belonging*, Routledge, London and New York.

Heryanto, Ariel and Vedi R Hadiz 2005, 'Post-authoritarian Indonesia: a comparative Southeast Asian perspective', *Critical Asian Studies* 37(2).

Hill, D 2007, 'Manoeuvres in Manado: media and politics in regional Indonesia', *South East Asia Research* 15(1).

HRW (Human Rights Watch) 2001, 'Indonesia: investigate death of Papuan leader,' press release, New York 11 November,www.hrw.org/press/2001/11/indonesia1111.htm

—— 2002, 'Indonesia: investigate shootings in Papua, no reprisals,' press release, New York, 5 September, www.hrw.org/press/2002/09/papua0905.htm

ICG 2002, *Indonesia briefing*, International Crisis Group, Jakarta/Brussels, 21 May 2002.

IFES 2005, *Public Opinion Survey Indonesia 2005*, International Foundation for Election Systems, Jakarta.

Jakarta Post 2000, 'VP advises Irianese to rethink freedom calls,' online, 18 September.

Janda, Kenneth 1980, *Political parties: a cross-national survey*, Free Press, New York.

Jenkins, David 1984, *Suharto and his generals: Indonesian military politics, 1975–1983*, Modern Indonesia Project, Cornell University, Ithaca.

Jurriëns, Edwin 2008, 'Television dreams: simulation, for a new reality of Indonesia' in Heryanto, A (ed), *Popular culture in Indonesia*, Routledge, London.

Kadane, Kathy 2003, 'The US government and CIA destroyed the PKI', *Tempo*, 10 June, www.tempo.co.id/majalah/arsip/2jp/jap05/lit-2.html.

Kahin, Audrey R and George McT Kahin 1995, *Subversion as foreign policy: the secret Eisenhower and Dulles debacle in Indonesia*, New Press, New York.

Kammen, D 1995, 'Rehearsals for employment: Indonesian school kids on strike in the 1990s' *Indonesia*, 60 October.

Ketetapan Majelis Permusyawaratan Rakyat Republik Indonesia Nomor IV/ MPR/2000 tentang Rekomendasi Kebijakan Dalam Penyelenggaraan Otonomi Daerah, *Ketetapan-Ketetapan Majelis Permusyawaratan Rakyat Republik Indonesia Hasil Sidang Umum Tahunan MPR RI Tahun 2000, 18 Agustus 2000.*

Ketetapan Majelis Permusyawaratan Rakyat Republik Indonesia Nomor II/MPR/1978 tentang Pedoman Penghayatan dan Pengamalan Pancasila (Ekaprasetia Pancakarsa), www.mpr.go.id/pdf/ketetapan /ketetapan%20mpr%20thn%2078.pdf

Kim YC, W Liddle and S Said 2006, 'Political leadership and civilian supremacy in third wave democracies: comparing South Korea and Indonesia', *Pacific Affairs* 79(2).

King, Dwight Y 2003, *Half-hearted reform: electoral institutions and the struggle for democracy in Indonesia*, Praeger, Westport/Connecticut and London.

Koentjaraningrat 1975.

Kompas 1995, 'Mayoritas Rakyat Indonesia belum merdeka dari Rasa Takut', 30 September, www.library.ohiou.edu/indopubs/1995/09/30/008.html

Kompas Cyber Media 2001a, 'Malam ini Provinsi Irian Jaya Disahkan Menjadi Provinsi Papua', 22 October.

Kompas Cyber Media 2001b, 'Theys Meninggal, Irian Berduka,' 12 November.

Kurniawan, Moch N 2003, 'Polls to disappoint reformists', *Jakarta Post*, 23 December.

Laksamana 2001, 'Violent affront: a chronology of FPI attacks', editorial, *Laksamana. net*, 16 October 2001

Lane, Max 2002, 'Globalizing debate on IMF: enter Indonesia', *Jakarta Post* editorial, 19 June.

Lev, Daniel 2005, 'Conceptual filters and obfuscation in the study of Indonesian politics', *Asian Studies Review*, 29 December.

Liddle, William R 1970, *Ethnicity, party, and national integration: an Indonesian case study*, Yale University Press, New Haven.

—— 1997, 'Coercion, co-optation and the management of ethnic relations in Indonesia' in Brown, Michael E and Sumit Ganguly (eds), *Government policies and ethnic relations in Asia and the Pacific,* MIT Press, Cambridge.

Liddle, William and Saiful Mujani 2000, 'The triumph of leadership: explaining the 1999 Indonesian vote', paper presented to the Association of Asian Studies Annual Meeting in San Diego, 9–12 March 2000. Copy obtained from one of the authors.

Linz, Juan J and Alfred Stepan 1996, 'Towards consolidated democracies', *Journal of Democracy*, 7(2).

LSI 2007, 'Parpol Tak Wakili Aspirasi Rakyat', Lembaga Survei Indonesia, 23 March.

—— 2008, 'Silent Revolution: Media dan Kekuatan Parpol Menuju Pemilu 2009', Lembaga Survei Indonesia, 16 October.

Mackie, JAC 1974, *Konfrontasi: the Indonesia–Malaysia Dispute 1963–1966*, Oxford University Press, Kuala Lumpur.

—— 2007, 'Australia and Indonesia: current problems, future prospects', Lowy Institute for International Policy, Double Bay.

Magnis-Suseno, Franz 1999, '*Langsir Keprabon*: New Order leadership, Javanese culture, and the prospects for democracy in Indonesia', in Forrester, Geoff 1999, *Post-Soeharto Indonesia: Renewal or Chaos?*, ISEAS, Singapore.

Mainwaring, Scott P 1999, *Rethinking party systems in the third wave of democratization: the case of Brazil*, Stanford University Press, Stanford.

Megawati Sukarnoputri 1999, speech, Singapore, 15 March 1999.

Merkel, Wolfgang 1998, 'The consolidation of post autocratic democracies: a multi-level model', *Democratization*, 5(3).

Michels, Robert 1959, *Political parties: a sociological study of the oligarchical tendencies of modern democracy*, Dover Publications, New York.

Mietzner, Marcus 2006, 'Ineffective electoral threshold needs reform', *Jakarta Post*, 14 December 2006.

—— 2007, 'Party financing in post-Soeharto Indonesia: between state subsidies and political corruption', *Contemporary Southeast Asia*, 29(2).

Mortimer, Rex (ed) 1974, *Showcase state: the illusion of Indonesia's 'accelerated modernization'*, Angus & Robertson, Brisbane.

Namier, Lewis 1962, 'Nationality and liberty' in *Vanished supremacies: essays on European history 1812–1918*, Penguin Books, Harmondsworth.

NDIIA (National Democratic Institute for International Affairs) 2000, *Indonesia's road to constitutional reform: the 2000 MPR Annual Session*, 12 October, www.accessdemocracy.org/library/1077_id_constireform.pdf

Nishimura, Shigeo 1995, 'The development of Pancasila moral education in Indonesia', *Southeast Asian Studies* 33(3).

Nordholt, Henk Schulte and Gerry van Klinken 2007, 'Introduction' in Nordholt and Klinken (eds), *Renegotiating boundaries: local politics in post-Soeharto Indonesia* KITLV Press, Leiden.

Paley, Julia 2002, 'Toward an anthropology of democracy', *Annual Review of Anthropology* 31.

Panebianco, Angelo 1988, *Political parties: organization and power*, Cambridge University Press, Cambridge.

Parker, Lynette 1992, 'The quality of schooling in a Balinese village', *Indonesia* 54.

Pemberton 2000, 'Formen der javanischen Pilgerschaft zu Heiligenschreinen', PhD thesis, Albert- Ludwigs- Universität Freiburg.

Pidato Ketua Umum DPP PDI Megawati Sukarnoputri Menjambut HUT ke XXV PDI', *SiaR* 11 January 1998.

Platzdasch, Bernhard 2001, 'Radical or reformist? How Islamic will the new movements make Indonesia?' *Inside Indonesia*, Oct–Dec.

Pompe, Sebastiaan 1999, *De Indonesische algemene verkiezingen 1999*, KITLV Uitgeverij, Leiden.

—— 2005, *The Indonesian Supreme Court: a study of institutional collapse*, Cornell Southeast Asia Program, Ithaca.

Pringgodigdo, AK 1957, *The office of President in Indonesia as defined in the three constitutions in theory and practice*, Modern Indonesia Project, Cornell University, Ithaca.

Rais, M Amien 1994, 'Suksesi 1998: suatu keharusan' [Succession in 1998: a must], in *Sintesis* 9(2) June–July, Center for Information and Development Studies, Jakarta.

Ramage, Douglas E 1995, *Politics in Indonesia: democracy, Islam, and the ideology of tolerance*, Routledge, London.

Randall, Vicky 1988, 'Conclusion', in Randall, Vicky (ed), *Political parties in the Third World*, SAGE Publications, London and Newbury Park.

—— 2006, *Party institutionalization and its implications for democracy*, paper presented at the IPSA Congress at Fukuoka, 9–13 July.

Randall, Vicky and Lars Svåsand 2001, 'Party institutionalisation and the new democracies' in Haynes, Jeff (ed), *Democracy and political change in the 'Third World'*, Routledge, London and New York.

Randall, Vicky and Lars Svåsand 2002a, 'Party institutionalization in new democracies', *Party Politics* (8)1.

Randall, Vicky and Lars Svåsand 2002b, 'Introduction: the contribution of parties in democracies and democratic consolidation', *Democratization*, 9(3).

Ravenhill, John 2002, 'Allies but not friends: the economic relationship', *Australian Journal of International Affairs* 55(2).

Reid, Anthony 1997, 'Entrepreneurial minorities, nationalism and the state', in Chirot, Daniel and Anthony Reid, *Essential outsiders: Chinese and Jews in the modern transformation of Southeast Asia and Central Europe*, University of Washington Press, Seattle.

Reuter, Thomas A 2003, *Inequality, crisis and social change in Indonesia*, Routledge-Curzon Press, London and New York.

Rieffel, Lex 2008, 'Indonesia's democracy lessons', www.brookings.edu/opinions/2008/0131_suharto_rieffel.aspx, 31 January.

Roosa, John 2006, *Pretext for mass murder: the September 30th movement and Suharto's coup d'etat in Indonesia*, University of Wisconsin Press, Madison.

Sabine, George H 1938, *A history of political theory*, Henry Holt and Company, New York.

Sambutan Ketua Umum DPP PDI Megawati Sukarnoputri pada Seminar Sehari Balitbang DPP PDI, Hotel Gran Melia, Jakarta, 28 September 1998, www.library. ohiou.edu/indopubs/1998/10/06/0004.html

Schwarz, Adam 1994, *A nation in waiting: Indonesia in the 1990s*, Allen & Unwin, Sydney.

Sen, Amartya 1999, *Development as freedom*, Random House, New York.

Sen, Krishna and David Hill 2000, *Media, culture and politics in Indonesia*, Oxford University Press, Melbourne.

Shi, T 2000, 'Political culture: a prerequisite for democracy?', *American Asian Review* 18(2).

Sinar Harapan 2003, '"Gelar Pahlawan" bagi Pelanggar HAM', 29 April 2003, www. sinarharapan.co.id/

Singh, Bilveer 2000, *Succession politics in Indonesia: the 1998 presidential elections and the fall of Suharto*, Macmillan Press, Hampshire.

Sjafri Sairin 1996 'Demokrasi dalam Perspektif Kebudayaan Minangkabau' [Democracy from the perspective of Minangkabau culture] in Najib, Muhammad (ed), *Demokrasi dalam Perspektif Budaya Nusantara* [Democracy in the Perspective of Indonesian Cultures], LKPSM, Yogyakarta.

Sjamsuddin, Nazaruddin 1996, 'Masyarakat Aceh dan Demokrasi' [Aceh society and democracy] in Najib, Muhammad (ed), *Demokrasi dalam Perspektif Budaya Nusantara* [Democracy from the perspective of Indonesian cultures], LKPSM, Yogyakarta.

Slatter, Dan 2006, 'The ironies of instability in Indonesia', *Social Analysis*, 50(1).

Straits Times 2002, Singapore, 16 June.

Stubbs, R 2001, 'Performance legitimacy and "soft authoritarianism"' in Acharya, A, BM Folic, and R Stubbs (eds), *Democracy, human rights, and civil society in Southeast Asia*, Joint Centre for Asia Pacific Studies, Toronto.

Suara Merdeka 2002, 'Ryamizard Hari Ini KSAD', online, 4 June.

Suara Pembaruan 1999, 'Wapres: Tanpa Irian Indonesia tidak Komplet,', www. library.ohiou.edu/indopubs/1999/12/15/0101.html, 14 December.

Sugiarto, Bima Arya 2006, *Beyond formal politics: party factionalism and leadership in post-authoritarian Indonesia*, PhD thesis, Australian National University.

Sukarno, *Suatu Bangsa jang Besar tidak akan Tenggelam,ketjuali djikalau Robek-robek Petjah dirinja sendiri dari Dalam: Amanat Presiden pada Peringatan Isra' dan Mir'radj pada Tanggal 21 Nopember 1965 di Istana Negara*, Djakarta, Departemen Penerangan, Indonesia.

Sukma, Rizal 2008, 'The quiet achiever: Islam, democracy and Indonesia's response to terrorism', Henry Jackson Society, www.henryjacksonsociety.org, 17 December.

Tan, Paige Johnson 2004, 'Party rooting, political operators and instability in Indonesia: a consideration of party system institutionalization in a communally charged society', paper presented to the Southern Political Science Association, New Orleans, Louisiana, 10 January.

Tempo Interaktif 2002, 'Ryamizard Dilantik sebagai KSAD', 4 June.

Tomsa, Dirk 2006, 'The defeat of centralized paternalism: factionalism, assertive regional cadres, and the long fall of Golkar Chairman Akbar Tandjung', *Indonesia*, 81 April.

—— 2007, 'Party politics and the media in Indonesia: creating a new dual identity for Golkar', *Contemporary Southeast Asia* 29(1).

—— 2008, *Party politics and democratization in Indonesia: Golkar in the post-Suharto era*, Routledge, London and New York.

Tovar, Hugh 2003, 'The CIA did not do it', *Tempo,* 18 November, www.tempo.co.id/majalah/arsip/2nd/edition04/lit-3.html

Ufen, Andreas 2006, *Political parties in post-Suharto Indonesia: between politik aliran and 'Philippinisasi'*, German Institute of Global and Area Studies, Hamburg.

van Dijk, Kees 2001, *A country in despair: Indonesia between 1997-2000*, KITLV Press, Leiden.

Ward, Ken 2007, 'Dealing with a democratic Indonesia: the Yudhoyono years', Lowy Institute, Sydney.

Webber, Douglas 2006, 'A consolidated patrimonial democracy? Democratization in post-Suharto Indonesia', *Democratization*, 13(3).

Yusi, AP and GWL Setiyardi 2001, 'CIA & 1965 coup: a list behind the bloodbath', *Tempo*, 2–8 October.